DEAR SON

DEAR SON

A FATHER'S ADVICE ON BEING A MAN

DAVE BRUSKAS

Tyndale House Publishers, Inc.
Carol Stream, Illinois

Visit Tyndale online at www.tyndale.com.

Visit Resurgence online at www.theresurgence.com.

TYNDALE and Tyndale's quill logo are registered trademarks of Tyndale House Publishers, Inc.

Resurgence Publishing, Inc, the Resurgence "R," and the Resurgence wordmark are registered trademarks of Resurgence.

Designed by Daniel Farrell

Edited by Jane Vogel

Published in association with Resurgence Publishing, Inc., 1411 NW 50th St., Seattle, WA 98107.

The author has previously posted some of the ideas in this book in blog form in "How to Live in a Secular Culture" at http://theresurgence.com/2013/11 /17/how-to-live-in-a-secular-culture.

The stories about the author's family are factual. In some of the stories about other people, names and details have been changed to conceal identities. The stories about Donald and Laura (page 50), Dan (page 55), Adam (page 115), and Nick (pages 140–141) are composite sketches based on trends the author has witnessed in ministry over several decades.

Library of Congress Cataloging-in-Publication Data

Bruskas, David.
    Dear son : a father's advice on being a man / David Bruskas.
        ISBN 978-1-4143-8971-4 (sc)
    1. Men (Christian theology) I. Title.
        BT703.5.B78 2014
        248.8'42—dc23   2014004743

Printed in the United States of America.

20	19	18	17	16	15	14
7	6	5	4	3	2	1

CONTENTS

FOREWORD

You do not have many fathers.

—1 CORINTHIANS 4:15

GOD IS A FATHER.

He loves us with fatherly affection and pursues us with fatherly devotion.

The Father's desire is that men would have his heart for both their family and their church family. At the end of the last book of the Old Testament, one of the final things God had to say for some four hundred years was that through repentance of sin and faith in Jesus Christ, the Son of the Father, God "will turn the hearts of fathers to their children and the hearts of children to their fathers" (Malachi 4:1-6). One significant aspect of God's work is different kinds of fathers who have different kinds of sons and daughters.

In our day, the lack of fathers with the Father's heart has become an epidemic. Homes are filled with sons who do not have fathers. And churches are filled with sons of God who do not have earthly spiritual fathers. The results are well known and widespread. The answer for many, if not most, of the problems in the church and culture is for biological fathers to love their biological sons, and spiritual fathers to love their spiritual sons.

We see this played out in the Bible. There we read of a fatherless son named Timothy who was spiritually adopted by a sonless father named Paul. Their relationship is a model for what spiritual fathering should be like, according to God our Father. Their relationship is the heart of this biblical, practical, hopeful book.

Curiously, Pastor Dave's story is somewhat like Paul's. Pastor Dave and his wonderful wife, Kara, have four beautiful daughters, but no living sons. They had a son, but he died in infancy, as you will read about in this book. That loss has profoundly shaped my friend. Every time I walk into his office, I see the picture of his little boy on his desk. On a trip together to Dallas along with our fellow executive elder, Pastor Sutton Turner, we stopped by the grave of his son to weep and pray together as fathers. Every year I pray for Pastor Dave and his family, as his son's birthday is the same as mine, and I wish I knew him and could celebrate with him.

Rather than being embittered against the Father over the loss of his son, Pastor Dave has embraced the Father's heart and invested his life in spiritual sons. We labor together for the family at Mars Hill Church, which is filled with newly converted young men suffering from a gaping hole in their life that should have been filled by a father. I asked Pastor Dave to write this book to help older men become better fathers and younger men become better sons. He has been teaching this content for many years to many men of many ages, races, and life stages. It was the core of his graduate studies at Dallas Seminary, the core of his leadership development in multiple churches where he has pastored, and the core of the development of the Mars Hill lead pastors who lead our network of churches. These men very gratefully sit down with Pastor Dave week after week and walk through the sections of Scripture regarding Timothy and Paul. Each man reports that this exercise is their favorite aspect of spiritual development and among the most valuable spiritual deposits anyone has ever made in them.

I am deeply thankful for the Father's heart I see in Pastor Dave. *Dear Son* is a great book, written by a great man, to meet a great need.

Pastor Mark Driscoll

INTRODUCTION

What I Wish I Could Say to My Son Now

February 17, 2013

Dear Son,

The last guests left the reception after your big sister Lisa's wedding a few hours ago. It's very early Sunday morning, but I can't sleep. I'm going through my mental photo album of the events of a day I will remember for the rest of my life. There's just so much to take in on a day like this. It makes me wish it could last a little longer.

David, you should have seen Lisa. She was beautiful and radiant and happy. As the doors swung open for me to walk her down the aisle, I started to weep. I wasn't sad about her marrying Tobin. I wish you could meet him. He is a solid man who loves Jesus, loves Lisa, and fits right into our sorority of a family with your three little sisters. I think I cried because the time Lisa spent in my life as my little girl had passed way too fast for my liking.

It reminds me of the very brief time you and I had together. Two months and four days were all we got, every minute within the four walls of the ICU at Children's Hospital. There were so many surgeries and procedures and shots and tubes and prayers and tears. We went from superhopeful to moderately hopeful to hopeless. But our time together during those sixty-four short days has given me a lifetime of memories to review. We had a deep father-and-son connection, and I vividly remember my time with you, and will for the rest of my life, much like I will remember Lisa's wedding.

Son, I cry a lot for a grown man. Especially as I grow older. At first it was embarrassing, but not so much anymore. I cry watching movie trailers, hearing the national anthem played at ball games, singing every Sunday in worship, and mostly when talking about you around the family dinner table. Lisa even broke down and cried a few weeks before her wedding because she wanted you to be there on her big day. She misses you. Your mom misses you. Lauren, Jennifer, and Jillian miss you. We all do.

There's rarely an hour that passes that I don't think about you. I dream about what you might look like if you were with us and how you would get along with all the girls in our home. I imagine us going on father-and-son outings, hanging out together while the Bruskas ladies shop, and cheering together as the

Cowboys disappoint us season after season. (That's a family tradition handed down to you through three generations.) But I mostly rehearse the conversations I think we would have.

Son, as you would be twenty-two this October, I think about all the things I would need to teach you about what it means to be a man. This is a crazy, confused world. It is very difficult for young men to live for Jesus. Many of your peers not only don't have Christian dads to teach them about life but don't have dads at all. While I know the opportunity for me to teach you about being a man in this life will never come, since you are now with Jesus and have a much better knowledge of him than I do, I wanted to write down the lessons I would have shared with you. Hopefully, some of these lessons can help men who don't have dads of their own.

I look forward to our reunion. Your mom had a big gift from God a couple of years ago. She saw you in a vision, as a young man, worshiping Jesus with your sisters. She smiled, then cried and almost fainted. She said you looked tall and thin, with brown, wavy hair and seemed very happy to be with Jesus. That sounds about right to me. I've asked for the same gift but haven't received it yet. Nonetheless, I know where you are and who you are with. The Bible says, "Faith is the assurance of things hoped for, the conviction of things not seen" (Hebrews 11:1).

I'm glad you are with Jesus. But I'm also glad you
still are with us in a significant way. I find comfort in
knowing you still are making a difference in my life and
hopefully in the lives of many young men who need a
spiritual dad to care for them. I'm always pleasantly
surprised how Jesus uses a sonless father like me
to teach fatherless sons. And all this began with your
short but meaningful life here with us. Thanks to Jesus
and thank you.

For Jesus' fame,
Dad

. . .

As I write these words, almost twenty-two years after David's
death, I find myself resonating more and more with the
apostle Paul's perspective on true and loved sons found in
his letters to Timothy and Titus. What follows in this book
are the letters I wish I could have written to my son if he were
still with us. Though David can't receive them here and now,
my hope is that my fatherly heart somehow will come out
and that I can encourage the other young men to whom I've
had the privilege of being a spiritual father. I think of Mario,
who was a non-Christian, single, impoverished, and broken
young man when he began attending the church I pastored.
Now he is married, has a daughter of his own, believes in
Jesus, and runs his own business. I am reminded of Los, who
was called by Jesus to plant a church. I am so proud of all

that he is doing to make a difference in his city. I also think of Justin, who came very close to believing in Jesus and then just vanished one day. He is most likely dead, and I often am haunted by his absence.

I am intrigued by Paul's inspired words to help younger men live for Jesus in a challenging world. I find that more and more young men are much like Timothy when he received Paul's letters; Dad is missing from their faithful legacy. I'm deeply grateful for the fatherless sons who have trusted me to be a spiritual father to them.

I wonder what Paul would say to Timothy today. If I can take what he wrote in 1 Timothy 4:12—"Let no one despise you for your youth, but set the believers an example in speech, in conduct, in love, in faith, in purity"—and through the help of the Holy Spirit, transfer it to fatherless young men in the form of some letters to my son, David, perhaps a few lives will be transformed and legacies altered.

1
CHRISTIAN

October 11, 2013

Dear Son,

Tonight we celebrated what would have been your
twenty-second birthday. I was on the road with your
older sister, Lisa, her husband, Tobin, and your younger
sisters Lauren and Jennifer in Lubbock, Texas. We had
a late night party at Chili's, complete with chips, salsa,
skillet cookies, and ice cream. It was an inexpensive
but fun evening. I think the waiter was hoping we
would rack up a bigger tab, but I tipped him well.
Your mom remained in Seattle with Jillian. They, too,
would have joined us so we could all be together, but
Jillian couldn't break free from her commitment as a
Roosevelt High School cheerleader. David, you would
be so proud of your sisters. They are smart, strong,
loving, and happy. They have become the young women
that I prayed they would be, which is a miracle in itself,

3

as I have been far from the perfect dad. I still don't understand women, but I am really thankful for them.

Your birthday is the hardest day of the year for our family each and every year. In a surprising way, it is far more difficult than the day that marks your death. It causes us to dream about what could have been if you were still with us today. We have a tradition on your birthday where each family member answers two questions: *What is your favorite memory of David?* and *What do you think he would be like if he were with us today?* I love how your three younger sisters, who never met you, talk about memories of you as if they were actually there while you were alive. I feel like your mom really has done a beautiful job of including them all in your life. We are very specific in our descriptions of what you would be like today. Everything from your height and weight and hair color to the clothes you would wear and the teams you would pull for. Everyone is convinced you would have been tall and thin with wavy brown hair. Your sisters think you would have liked music. We're all certain you would have been a die-hard Dallas Cowboys fan because that is a birthright in the Bruskas home. But who really knows for sure?

What I do know for sure is that we miss you so much. We each have an ache in our hearts that varies in pain but never goes away. Your birthday is a tough day. Mostly, we cry a lot. I always make sure to give your mom flowers. They remind her you are with Jesus and a reunion is coming someday.

Every year on this day, I also think about what I would have wanted for your life. The truth is, although I would have had many dreams and ambitions for you, I really would have wanted only one thing. I would have wanted you to be a man who lives for Jesus. Everything else is flexible and tends to fall into place when a man lives for Jesus. But even if everything seems to be going well for a man—except for knowing Jesus—life is empty and failed.

The apostle Paul tells his spiritual son, Timothy, "I long to see you, that I may be filled with joy. I am reminded of your sincere faith, a faith that dwelt first in your grandmother Lois and your mother Eunice and now, I am sure, dwells in you as well" (2 Timothy 1:4-5). I would love to say the same words to you. If you were still with us, I would want to know that such faith—the faith that dwelt in Kathleen, your great-grandmother; and in Tom and Betty and Dale and Mary, your grandparents; and in your mom and me; and dwells in your sisters, Lisa, Lauren, Jennifer, and Jillian— also would dwell in you and your children and your grandchildren. I would love to have seen you be another link in the chain of faith through generations of people who have our same last name!

Happy birthday, David! I miss you. There's not an hour that passes that I don't think about you. While

I want to live a long life if that helps your mom and your sisters, I will be more than ready when my time comes to join you and Jesus.

Until then, know I love you,

Dad

. . .

How is life working for you? Being a young man, as I recall (although it has been a while), is really very good. You are as energetic and strong as you will ever be. You are also free and unencumbered. Free to pursue the work of your choosing. Free to pursue women. Mostly free to live where you want and do what you want when you want. Free to pursue, as our Founding Fathers desired, life, liberty, and happiness. Right now, you are free to go after all that you want from the world. But what if your freedom is blinding you to what actually may be enslaving you? What if, in the energy and idealism of young manhood, you are in the process of losing the only thing that matters while chasing everything else? Jesus warned everyone, including young men, with this terrifying question: "What will it profit a man if he gains the whole world and forfeits his soul?" (Matthew 16:26).

I was more of a boy than a young man when I saw how empty life could be. I grew up in a very loving home. Both of my parents worked hard to provide for my needs. They also did everything they could to protect me from danger. They nurtured me and guided me toward a good and decent life.

But for the first eleven years of my life, my parents weren't Christians. And I'm sure I wasn't either.

We did attend church once or twice a year with my grandma. She would bribe us with the promise of an after-church brunch at her country club. My dad owned a small and struggling lumberyard, and my mom was a bookkeeper. They weren't country club material, so getting to go with Grandma was a real treat. I didn't like church, but pulling endless clumps of bacon from a silver tray using tongs was more than worth the hour of suffering I had to endure in church.

I found church to be creepy and confusing. The building's high ceilings, hidden balconies, tall curtains, dark corners, stained-glass windows, and musty, padded pews led me to think I was worshiping a ghostly god in his haunted house. The robed choir didn't help ease my fears. Worst of all were the bizarre sounds of the pipe organ, played loudly as if to summon the ghostly god to come out and haunt his houseguests.

To my juvenile mind, the point of all this seemed to be scaring me into living a good life so this god would bless me rather than punish me. I would be frightened into sharing with my little brother, telling grown-ups the truth, and making good grades in school. At least I would be for a week. Then I was supposed to come back the next Sunday, because the impact of church seemed to have a six-day shelf life. This was like a wash, rinse, and repeat cycle. It certainly wasn't my grandma's fault that I felt this way. Truthfully, it wasn't the church's fault either. I would find out later that my perception was really distorted. I was blind and deaf to what actually was happening.

My childhood was mostly happy. My dad loved sports, hunting, fishing, and most of all, his sons. So he religiously put together the things he loved, and we all had a great time, especially on weekends. My mom was caring, nurturing, and hardworking. She always made sure we were well prepared for each day. Our family was healthy in nearly every way but one: we were spiritually bankrupt. No matter how many things are right, if this one thing is wrong, everything else is too.

My dad was agnostic and was hostile toward religion. Mom considered herself a Christian because of her upbringing in church. She was mildly religious. But she seemed as uncomfortable at Grandma's church as the rest of us. Her life slowly was coming apart because of an alcohol addiction.

Mom was a binge drinker. I remember being at several parties with her as a child—parties that would end with Dad carrying her to the car as we left, suddenly and with much embarrassment. No one felt worse about this problem than Mom. So much so, that as she arrived one night at a New Year's Eve party, she began weeping even before she took her first drink. She knew what was coming: the night would end with her being carried to the car as a sloppy, drunken mess.

But this party *wouldn't* be like the others. This night would end very differently. Soon our whole family would change forever.

One of Mom's friends compassionately noticed her tears. This woman carefully listened to her story of shame. The woman then did something unexpected. She invited my mom to join her and some other women at a weekly meeting to study the Bible. Mom first went out of desperation. Desperation turned to hope as she grew to know the Jesus she had heard preached and sung about in church for most of her life. My mom became a Christian and was transformed. No more drinking binges. No more lampshade-wearing, vomit-soaked partying. No more shame and no more guilt. One change among all the others impressed me most. She loved my dad, my little brother, and me better than she had before. She always had been a kind and good mom, but now she was more loving and happier than before. But for me, at least, there was a huge downside to her conversion. My little brother, Bill, and I now had to go with her to church every Sunday instead of just twice a year. And there was no bonus of country-club bacon anymore.

We went to a lot of different churches. It seems as if we tried every one in town until Mom found one that she believed fit our family. My dad, as devoutly agnostic as one could be (it seems odd to be passionately certain about something you profess you aren't sure of), refused to go with us. He was my golden ticket out of church. As long as he held out, I knew I could miss a fair number of Sundays in the woods hunting, or at the lake fishing, or even yelling with him at the TV set as we watched the Dallas Cowboys.

Then, much to my dismay, he showed up at the breakfast

table one Sunday morning before church wearing his favorite powder-blue leisure suit. He announced, "If this is the only way I can spend time with my family on Sunday mornings, then I will go to church." My goal to be a casual and infrequent church attender was dashed. I wasn't happy. I couldn't hold out on church. But I certainly could hold out as long as needed to avoid becoming a Christian. Or so I thought.

I really don't exactly remember how long my dad attended church before he, too, became a Christian. I just recall being disappointed in how rapidly he went from being a religious agnostic to a born-again believer. Surprisingly, it wasn't going to church that led to his conversion. It was watching the television series *Jesus of Nazareth* that captured his heart. His conversion was every bit as dramatic as my mom's. If there was a single characteristic that defined his transformation—much like with Mom—it was the radical love he had for his family. It was a newer, deeper, more loyal and joyful love than we had ever seen before. This surprised me because I thought being a Christian was about doing all the right things while avoiding all the wrong things. I quickly learned it had much more to do with love. This wasn't a Hallmark-card, sticky-and-sloppy type of love but a sacrificial, active, and thick love. It was a love that looked like the type of love Jesus said he had for his disciples: "Greater love has no one than this, that someone lay down his life for his friends" (John 15:13). More than ever before, I saw the many ways my mom and dad sacrificed themselves for my brother and me. While I was very skeptical of their new beliefs, I was compelled by their new lifestyle.

After my parents became Christians, I began to feel pressure to become one too. Not so much from them. They made me go to church with them, but beyond talking a lot about the Bible and Jesus, they didn't force their beliefs on me. Yet every time I went to church, I felt a pull in the pit of my stomach, especially when the preacher would invite people to walk to the front of the sanctuary at the end of the service and publicly give their lives to Jesus. My prejudice—that Christianity was just another world religion to help people cope with the unanswerable questions about life and death—began to fade. To me, Christianity was becoming less about a philosophy or lifestyle and more and more about the person of Jesus, this man who claimed to be God, and who backed up his claim by rising from the dead. At least that's what those who believed in him told me.

The more pressure I felt to become a Christian, the stronger my resistance toward church grew. I took a flyer that was mailed to my house inviting me to a youth retreat and hid it in the trash. I knew my parents would make me go if they saw it. The day before the retreat began, I went to school confident I had succeeded. I would be shooting hoops with my unbelieving buddies while my churchy friends studied their Bibles on the retreat. While I was in class, my youth pastor called my parents to personally request that I attend. I came home to the bad news of my fate and two days later had the most profound conversation of my life.

Vern was a youth pastor from Missouri. He was leading my small group during the weekend retreat. He asked if we could meet one-on-one. I thought this request was really strange but agreed anyway. When we met, he opened up the Bible and with laser precision read verses that confirmed what I was beginning to understand about Jesus. He was real. He was God. He had unfinished business with me. He wanted to forgive me for all my active and passive rebellion. He wanted to free me to live my life for him moving forward. I felt two strong, paradoxical emotions simultaneously. On one hand, I had the deepest remorse for resisting this Jesus who had pursued me. I realized I was responsible for his brutal death. I was cut to the heart. Strangely, at the very same time, I felt Jesus loved me rather than hated me and would accept me. I also felt he could change me. He was going to give me a new life instead of killing me for opposing him. That's exactly what he did!

With Vern right there with me, I prayed to Jesus. I told Jesus I wanted to be forgiven and freed. I told him I hated my sin and wanted to leave it all behind. I also told him I loved him and wanted to follow him for the rest of my life. On Saturday evening, March 10, 1979, I turned from sin and trusted in the person and work of Jesus. I was born again. I was converted.

A change of heart and mind came upon me at the very same time in life that my voice and body were changing, my very own mid-puberty conversion. Both were drastic. I quickly grew to love the Bible. I read it every chance I could get. I loved my family more than I ever had before. I even loved my little brother. I really loved telling my friends who didn't know Jesus about him. And some of them, too, met Jesus just as I had.

I also began to love the church. I loved being in worship services and now understood what was happening. I loved being with other Christians and hearing about what Jesus was doing in their lives. Probably more than anything else, I enjoyed connecting my friends who didn't yet know Jesus with those who already did.

Maybe you have a loving father who brought you to church and sent you on Christian retreats. But please don't feel a sense of hopelessness if your biological father *hasn't* helped you to meet Jesus. Maybe you don't have a reliable earthly father who loves Jesus. Maybe you don't have a reliable earthly father *period*. You may have nothing but a legacy of wrongs, losses, and pain. But there is hope for you to meet Jesus and become the man he calls you to be, even if you lack a positive legacy and a good biological father. Timothy, from the Bible, found such a man in Paul.

Timothy was raised in an ancient city called Lystra, in modern-day Turkey. Acts 16 mentions that his mother was a devout Jewish Christian. All we know about Timothy's dad is that he was ethnically a Greek. There is no mention of his faith. It would seem that Paul stepped in and took on the spiritual responsibility that was entrusted to Timothy's biological dad. We read in the Bible that Timothy and Paul were very close. It is quite possible that Paul led Timothy to Jesus. It also is a possibility that Timothy, as a young man, watched his spiritual father being stoned by an angry mob. Left to die,

Paul miraculously recovered and continued on with his ministry. (You can read about that in Acts 14:19-21.) Imagine the trauma and emotional scars young Timothy would have felt! His biological dad wasn't helpful, and Timothy almost lost the man who was most helpful to him to a murderous mob. That sounds much like the pain I find in so many young men today.

Max grew up in a rough part of town, without a dad. He soon found an alternative to his dysfunctional family in a street gang. Young manhood began for Max before he even became a teenager. He was dealing drugs and having sex by the time he was twelve years old. He became a cocaine addict. When I first met Max, he already was stricken with AIDS, was in the throes of addiction, and had children of varying ages with several ex-girlfriends. I've seen few lives that were worse than Max's. But then Max met Jesus. And his life, although far from perfect, is being reshaped and redeemed. He's beginning to see God as his true Father. And as he relates to God as his Father, Max is becoming a father to his children.

John best could be described as a good kid. His mom and dad split up when he was young. He still has contact with his dad but receives very little spiritual support from him. His mom remarried, and John's stepdad is more religious than helpful toward his stepson. Jesus has interrupted John's life much as he did Max's. Now, although John still lives with the pain of his biological dad's not being a spiritual father to him, he is learning through Jesus to be the dad, biologically and spiritually, he wishes his father had been to him.

Paul's greatest gift to Timothy wasn't being a surrogate father through good deeds. He wasn't a big brother or a recovery sponsor. He was way more than that. Paul's best gift to young Timothy was being his spiritual father through the gospel of Jesus. *Gospel*, as you may know, literally means *Good News*. Much like Paul, I believe what young men like Timothy— and you—need today is Good News from God.

> The saying is trustworthy and deserving of full acceptance, that Christ Jesus came into the world to save sinners.
> —1 Timothy 1:15

The essence of the gospel message and the most important thing I can teach you is summed up best by the apostle Paul to Timothy in this statement: "The saying is trustworthy and deserving of full acceptance, that Christ Jesus came into the world to save sinners, of whom I am the foremost" (1 Timothy 1:15). If you forget everything else I tell you, make sure you remember that verse. The gospel is most basically the great news that **Jesus saves sinners**. Let me unpack that for you word by word in reverse order.

- **Sinners:** You and I and everyone else who has ever been born are sinners by nature and by choice. That's not a popular notion in our culture, but we are born guilty of treason against the very God who created us. Our common forefather, Adam, represented the entire human race before the God who created us all. Adam sinned against God by disobeying God's only prohibitive order. So the tragic and cosmic result is that we inherit Adam's guilt along with his rebellious nature toward God. We also inherit his death sentence of eternal separation from God.

To further our misery, we continue to live out of our instinctive nature as sinners. According to the Bible, we are born idolaters. We worship the created world, and most commonly ourselves, rather than the God who made us to worship him. Our ears are deaf, our eyes are blind, and our hearts are dead toward God. So we hopelessly continue down the path of rebellion. God is right to be angry with us as we all oppose his rule. There is nothing whatsoever we can do to change ourselves that will lead him to change his mind about us. But God *can* change his mind, and he did. He sent his Son, Jesus, on a rescue mission to save sinners from the power and penalty of sin.

- **Jesus Saves:** The God of the Bible is triune. He is one God in three persons: Father, Son, and Spirit. Each person of the Godhead is coeternal, without beginning. Each person of the Godhead is coequal and coworthy of worship. Each person of the Godhead is coexistent, living eternally in perfect relationship with honor, love, and esteem for one another. But each person of the Godhead plays a different role in saving sinners. The Bible teaches us that God the Father sent God the Son on a mission to save sinners. God the Spirit breathes new life into dead human hearts so they turn from sin and trust in God the Son.

Jesus—God the Son—entered our world as a human. Much like Adam, he represented the entire human race before God. He was like us in every way except one: he didn't inherit Adam's guilt and sinful nature, so he never rebelled against God his Father. Jesus wasn't a sinner by nature *or* by choice. Through the empowerment of God the Spirit, Jesus lived the only perfect life that ever has been lived. Jesus died the death we deserve. He died on the cross, the perfect God-man taking our sin upon himself and paying the penalty we deserve. He was buried. Then three days later, just as he had promised, he physically rose from the dead. Within weeks, after being with his followers, he ascended into a realm known as heaven.

Jesus has made it possible, through his perfect life, his sacrificial death, and his victorious resurrection, for you and me and anyone else who trusts in him to be forgiven from the penalty of sin and freed from the enslaving power of sin. This is the great news of God through Jesus: Jesus saves sinners.

The question then arises, *What can we do about it? How can we be saved?*

Tragically, this is where so many people get it wrong. There are basically two ways to respond to Jesus' rescue mission. The Bible divides these paths into the categories of law and grace.

To respond to Jesus by the law is a futile attempt to bridge the chasm that exists between God and us by keeping rules. In this sense, a person becomes righteous by keeping the commands (613 in total) recorded in the Old Testament. While this approach *sounds* noble, it is terribly ineffective and devastatingly useless.

I remember Ryan, who showed up at the church I was pastoring some time back. I really enjoyed the friendship we developed. But Ryan never grasped how to relate to God through Jesus. He loved to say, "Pastor Dave, to be a Christian, you have to want it, work hard to get it, and work even harder to keep it." In other words, Ryan thought the path to Jesus was about doing certain things that were good while avoiding things that were bad. It was all about what we do for Jesus instead of what Jesus has done for us.

According to Paul's warning in another letter, that was never the purpose of the law. Paul states, "By works of the law no human being will be justified in [God's] sight, since through the law comes knowledge of sin" (Romans 3:20). In other words, this legalistic approach never works. Here's why: the law can't make us right and acceptable to God. It does have a good purpose if understood correctly. It can make it obvious to us that we need an obedience we don't have and can't attain. The law can lead us to the reality that we really need Jesus.

Jesus' obedience, resulting in his right and perfect standing before God, is offered to us as a free gift. It is gratis, the truest and freest gift, because righteousness is offered to those who least deserve it. This is what the Bible refers to as grace.

Again, God does for us in Jesus what we never could do for ourselves. The law guides us, if used correctly, to the desperate awareness that we need grace.

When I first came to Jesus, I had a bad temper. And since I have known him, he has helped me grow in this area. But I still have a ways to go. I knew before I was a Christian that it was wrong to kill someone. Although the idea had crossed my mind, I never acted on it. But I had many fistfights with my little brother, my friends, and neighborhood kids. I knew one of the Ten Commandments was "You shall not murder" (Exodus 20:13). But when I read Jesus' words, I realized I was already guilty: "You have heard that it was said to those of old, 'You shall not murder; and whoever murders will be liable to judgment.' But I say to you that everyone who is angry with his brother will be liable to judgment; whoever insults his brother will be liable to the council; and whoever says, 'You fool!' will be liable to the hell of fire" (Matthew 5:21-22). Right there in red print in my Bible I was condemned to hell! I hadn't killed anyone, but I was angry with my brother and had called him worse things than a fool. And no matter how resolved I was never to do it again, it was too late. I was guilty. And I needed Jesus to take away my guilt and give me in its place his obedience to this law. And that is exactly what he did!

The Bible is clear: we receive the amazing gift of salvation

> *If you forget everything else, remember this: Christ Jesus came into the world to save sinners.*

19

by grace *through* repentance and faith (see 2 Corinthians 7:10; Ephesians 2:8). Repentance is turning from sin with our whole being: *intellectually knowing* that independence toward God is loathsome to him, *emotionally feeling* that God has been greatly offended, and *willfully choosing* to turn away from sin as an exercise of the will. To repent literally means to turn away from something. It means to change. It's like when a child accidentally follows someone he thinks is his dad in the supermarket, realizes the man he's following isn't his dad, and turns from that man toward the man who is his father. In this way, repentance is turning away from following sin and turning toward our Father God through Jesus.

Hand in hand with repentance must come faith. Faith is trusting in God and his reliability to say what he means and mean what he says. Faith also is trusting entirely in the finished work of Jesus for the forgiveness and freedom from sin.

So What Now?

I don't want you to be like my mom in understanding grace. She was surrounded by the gospel message yet had not received its great offer of grace. She was working toward being a better person, being more religious, and doing good works. But she still was brutally enslaved by the power of sin and obligated to pay its horrific penalty. She was blind to see and deaf to hear grace. That's when Jesus stepped in and saved a sinner. He showed her all her sin, broke her heart, and then gave her a brand-new one.

I also don't want you to be like my dad. He was so lost. He believed all religions were the same and therefore equally futile. From his perspective, all that mattered was the here and now. But Jesus stepped into my dad's life unannounced as well. Even though my dad didn't get it for years, he, too, was blind to see and deaf to hear grace. In a different way than my mom, he was working toward being a better person through his own religion of unbelief and good works. While he didn't live to please God, he did try to live a good life to help himself and others. But despite his very best efforts, he was empty in a way he couldn't change. He, much like his alcoholic wife, was brutally enslaved to a life of rebellion against God. Then Jesus broke my dad's old heart and gave him a whole new one.

Mostly I don't want you to be like me before I met Jesus. I watched those around me being transformed, yet I fought the tug I felt on my own heart. I have a simple warning for you: resistance is futile. It's time to give up and give in to Jesus' working on your heart. It's time to repent. Turn from sin and trust in Jesus. Become the man you were created to be. Join the legacy of faith that exists for those who trust in Jesus. If you have grown up without a spiritual mentor or a legacy of faith, begin a new legacy today by being the first of many who believe and obey Jesus!

We don't need to become *better* men to become Christians. We need to become *new* men. Jesus refers to this as being born again (see John 3:3). The big idea is that something radical happens to us that we can't make happen for ourselves.

We can't make ourselves be born again any more than we can make ourselves be born in the first place. But God wants us to be born again. And he *is* able to give us new lives. He does so through the third person of the Trinity, the Holy Spirit. I believe you are reading this book because God desires to give you the gift of repentance and faith so that you might become a new man. And as you read this, the Holy Spirit may be working in you.

If so, you likely are experiencing a couple of paradoxical things simultaneously. You are feeling a sense of remorse and guilt over your sin. You realize, perhaps for the first time, that you have lived independently and rebelliously toward the God who created you to worship him. But here is what likely feels strange: you feel this very same God reaching out to you in love through Jesus. He is offering to forgive you of sin and to free you to live a new life for him. And all that is left for you to do is receive his offer by turning from sin and trusting Jesus to forgive and free you.

When you become a new man, one who is transformed by Jesus and indwelt by the Holy Spirit, you will have at least three new dimensions. First, you will have a brand-new identity. According to the Bible, "If anyone is in Christ, the new creation has come: the old has gone, the new is here!" (2 Corinthians 5:17, NIV). As a Christian, you aren't an improved version of your old self; you are an entirely new man. Second, the new you will have new desires (see Romans 7:4-6, for instance). Practically, this means you will have a newfound hatred for rebellion against God and a new passion to worship him in everything he is and does. Last, you will have a new power to live according to your new identity and new desires. The Holy Spirit will empower you to live an obedient life (see Romans 8:9-13). Your new manhood will most be characterized by becoming a young man who thinks, feels, acts, and speaks like Jesus.

2
—
SON

Dear Son,

I will remember for the rest of my life the day you
were born. It was a nearly perfect day. A sunny, warm
October day in Dallas. As your mom and I drove into the
lot at Baylor Hospital, I was peaceful. This in itself was
a miracle. I was on the verge of a nervous breakdown
during the birth of your sister Lisa. Everything was new
and traumatic. But this time was different. We had a
better idea of what to expect. And we knew ahead of
time that you were a boy. The ultrasound revealed as
much. But we had no clue that your tiny heart would be
flawed and that your life with us would be over in two
short months. The ultrasound did not reveal that.

 We were checked into a labor room by late
afternoon and passed much of the evening, between
your mom's contractions, watching court hearings on

TV. Late on the evening of October 11, 1991, you were born into this world. Grandmas and grandpas, aunties and uncles were there to pay a visit. You were the most handsome baby I ever had seen. I loved you, just as I did Lisa, the moment I saw you. I was amazed at how quickly and deeply I could connect with someone I just had met for the first time. I instantly had that fatherly feeling. I sensed this was the very thing God made me to be: your dad.

All seemed well with the world as I lay in the sleeping chair next to your mom's hospital bed. The nurses moved you into the newborn nursery, and I fell into a tranquil and deep sleep. That lasted until your mom woke me a few hours later and asked me to go check on you. She was concerned because you hadn't been returned to her for nursing. So I sleepily made my way to the nursery.

I wasn't prepared for what I saw. I was redirected from the normal nursery to the pediatric intensive care unit. And there you lay, in a tiny little bed, your tiny chest heaving with each breath. I agonized as I watched you work to do what comes so naturally to most people that they aren't even aware it's happening. Were you traumatized by this harsh new world you'd entered? Were you frightened? I wanted badly to pick you up and comfort you. All I wanted to do was take you home with your mom, away from all the equipment and noise.

The nurses and doctors explained that you were struggling to get saturated oxygen into your bloodstream. They suspected you had a congenital heart defect, and they were making arrangements to transfer you to Children's Hospital for further diagnosis. Just like that, I was given the worst news I ever had heard. I slowly made my way back up to your mom's room to tell her that her greatest fear was now a reality: her little boy, her long-awaited son, a few hours old, wasn't healthy.

Leaving her in the hospital bed with tears streaming down her face in order to follow the ambulance to Children's Hospital was one of the hardest things I've ever done. I was torn: Should I stay with your mom or go with you? But she insisted I go. I was a young man then, just a few years into my twenties. I had just been gut punched by life. It hurt really, really bad. And it was very confusing. For the first time ever, I took a blow that knocked me down to my knees, and I couldn't seem to summon the strength to stand back up.

Something powerful happened during that fifteen-minute drive through the streets of downtown Dallas. I became your father in the fiercest way. I vowed to do everything in my power to fight for your life. That's exactly what I did for the next sixty-three days. Sixty-three days of sleeping in waiting rooms and hospital hallways, eating when possible but not regularly, agonizing with every downturn and exulting in every positive turn, and hardest of all, living mostly as part of a disconnected family doing shifts at the hospital. Those days were the most difficult days of my life. So difficult that I figured I had lost years of longevity and likely wouldn't live past forty. Then, after a gallant battle, you were taken from us to be with Jesus.

I loved you as I tracked you to the hospital with a wholehearted, forever-and-always kind of love. I love you every bit as much, actually more than then, today. I am your father and you are my son. Neither life nor death will ever change that.

For Jesus' fame,

Dad

. . .

Even though David and I spent only a short time together, I began to understand the importance of a healthy father-son relationship. Much of what it means to be a man is rooted in an identity as a son. The apostle Paul knew this to be true. He also understood how important it was to Timothy. (So much so, that he addresses him as both his "true child" and his "beloved child" in his letters to Timothy included in the Bible.) The world we live in is unstable and rough and can test a man to the limits of his strength. A man first discovers foundational strength and core stability in belonging to a loving father. A boy's very first identity upon birth is that of son. When a father loves and accepts his son, he enables his son to weather the trying storms of life in security. But if an absent or abusive dad rejects his son, that son very well may spend the rest of his life in an attempt to win his father's approval.

In this broken world full of imperfect fathers, I want you to know that to be a Christian is to be perfectly and totally loved. To be a Christian is to be born again—through the person and work of Jesus applied by the Holy Spirit—as a true son of the true Father. The Father loves you with all the love he has for his Son, Jesus. The Father says to his Son, Jesus, "You are my beloved Son; with you I am well pleased" (Mark 1:11). His love and pleasure are without limit. This love the Father has for the Son is the very same love the Father has for you when you become his child. You receive Jesus' perfect record and therefore are loved by the Father. Jesus plainly says it this way: "The Father himself loves you, because you have loved me and have believed that I came from God" (John 16:27). This is exactly what it

> To be a Christian is to be perfectly and totally loved.

looks like to live as a Christian young man. It's all about living in the love that the Father has for the Son, which is available to you in Jesus.

John, who wrote the Gospel bearing his name and followed Jesus for the entirety of his earthly ministry, declares that Jesus "came to his own, and his own people did not receive him. But to all who did receive him, who believed in his name, he gave the right to become children of God, who were born, not of blood nor of the will of the flesh nor of the will of man, but of God" (John 1:11-13).

At least two key points stand out to me in this incredible passage. First, the way to become a child of God, his son, is through receiving Jesus by believing in all he says he is. (That's what is meant by the phrase "believed in his name.") Second, you become God's child by his will. You don't become his son because he needs you in some way. You don't become his son because you finally come to your senses and make a good decision. You become his son because he loves you and wants you to be his. You become a son of the Father through his good intention. It is his will.

All us of need an identity upon which to build the foundation of our lives. Your first identity as a Christian young man is to be the true son of your heavenly Father through Jesus. There is nothing more powerful than walking through the peaks and valleys of life knowing God has made you his son through Jesus—simply because he wanted to. The love you find in this position, being a beloved son of God, will do more to free you from sin and the resulting shame and guilt than anything else or anyone else anywhere.

You probably know men who go about life trying to win the love and approval of their earthly dads. They struggle with insecurity, striving to win the love of a father who is either distant or absent. These "fatherless" sons are very much like unanchored ships in a turbulent harbor, crashing into other ships, running ashore or crashing into the docks, only to then be washed out to sea. Maybe you feel that way. Be warned:

the damage you do can go far beyond yourself. Unanchored men often take women and children down with them as they sink in a deep ocean of despair. They leave behind a trail of broken and devastated lives.

My friend Larry was one of those "fatherless" men, even though his father was physically present. Larry was one of the most gifted basketball players I knew in high school. We played together, and I knew to pass him the ball if I wanted to win a game. He could score from anywhere on the court. Larry was motivated by an alcoholic dad who never seemed to be pleased with his son's play. The better Larry performed on the court, the more demanding his dad became, until one season, Larry didn't try out for the team. He became an alcoholic just like his dad. He was broken and began to break others in the process.

Fatherless men often seem to be self-focused and self-serving. When you lack the freedom that comes from knowing your identity is rooted in something greater than anything on this earth, you can't give yourself away in sacrifice to the benefit of others. Self-sacrifice, instead of self-service, results mostly from being anchored in your identity as a beloved son of God. While it would be easy to be angry and even threatened by insecure young men and the wreckage they bring into our homes, workplaces, churches, and communities, I find their plight heartbreaking.

If you are one of these men, I want you to know about the hope you can find in Jesus. I want you to discover the family and the home you can find in his church. I want you to know that even if you have lived under the weight of an abusive, negligent, or absent earthly father, the heavenly Father waits eagerly for you to come home through Jesus. I want you to know and love Jesus. I want you to understand how deeply you are loved by God, your true and best Father, as his dear son. But you will never know and love Jesus unless you first understand God's deep love for you. And as you experience God's love for you in Jesus, I want you to be fearless. I want you to live in the power of the Holy Spirit. I want you to love like Jesus and live like Jesus.

How does God's love transform our lives? God's love is not simply touchy and feely. It's a strong love that dispels fear.

Even if you have lived under the weight of an abusive, negligent, or absent earthly father, the heavenly Father waits eagerly for you to come home through Jesus.

If I had the opportunity to discuss this with my son, I would turn to Paul's words to his spiritual son Timothy. According to Paul, there are big-time implications of this kind of love. Paul writes, "God gave us a spirit not of fear but of power and love and self-control" (2 Timothy 1:7). If I could take one thing away from you today and give you three things you might be lacking, I would take away your fear and give you power, love, and self-control.

I've seen young men in their twenties—many of whom have grown up without any strong father figures—let fear rule their lives. I think of Shawn, whose dad left Shawn's mom early in his life. Shawn felt that he never would be able to be a good husband and was sure to follow in his father's footsteps. So he was afraid to approach a woman he was interested in because he believed he ultimately would fail her, just as his dad had failed his mom. It doesn't have to be that way with you. True, if you reject God's love, you are right to be afraid. You are living in imminent danger—the worst kind of danger—you are living a breath away from the terrible wrath of God. But if you believe in Jesus, there is no place for any fear in your life. First John 4:18 reads, "There is no fear in love, but perfect love casts out fear." This type of love—perfect love—comes from God through Jesus: "In this is love, not that we have loved God but that he loved us and sent his Son to be the propitiation for our sins" (1 John 4:10). You are loved by God the Father, who sent his Son, Jesus, to be the propitiation (the one who received the penalty of God's terrible wrath) for our sins. You aren't loved conditionally or partially; you are loved perfectly and completely! When that kind of love fills your life, all fear vanishes. When fear disappears, some really good things begin to happen.

Not only does fear evaporate, but a new power also emerges. A power embodied in the presence of the Holy Spirit. A power that kills sin in the heart of its host. A power that helps you endure a hostile culture rife with suffering and hardship. A power that enables you to call out anytime, any-where, "Abba! Father!" (Romans 8:15). While it is true that you can cause devastating harm, just like those unanchored ships, it is equally true that when you live as a loved son of God in Jesus, yielded to the Holy Spirit, you have the potential for enormous positive impact.

Remember Shawn? As he began to understand, through the work of the Holy Spirit, that God is his true Father, he also began to realize that he can be like his heavenly Father. He wasn't destined to abandon his future wife. He could be like his real Father, who faithfully loves and never abandons or abuses his people. Shawn gained the courage to pursue the woman he admired. They now are married and have a daughter, and Shawn is a faithful husband and an attentive dad.

With this new power and a new identity activated by the Holy Spirit comes a new love, a love that is largely unfamiliar to many and certainly rare in our world. A love that is sacrificial. It is, in fact, the very love of Jesus for others. The love that he calls the greatest kind: "Greater love has no one than this, that someone lay down his life for his friends" (John 15:13). Nothing kills the imposter tyrant of self-focused, self-important, self-absorbed, and self-serving love more than the self-sacrificing love of Jesus pouring into our lives through the conduit of the Holy Spirit (see Romans 5:5).

My friend Abiel exhibits that kind of love. Abiel easily could find a job working in a church in his home nation of Mexico. He always has wanted to work full-time in a ministry position. But out of love for Spanish speakers living in the United States, Abiel pours long and hard hours into his own cleaning business so he can help an English-speaking church more effectively reach out to Mexican immigrants living in the same community. He does so sacrificially, but joyfully and powerfully! He hasn't literally died for others as Jesus did, but he has given up his dreams in order to help his friends.

The Holy Spirit can give you a new *power* for living like Jesus, a new *love* for loving like Jesus, and a new *self-control*. I know self-control is something that doesn't come naturally or easily. Idealism and impulsiveness are common traits for men in their college years and twenties—I know that's what I was like when I was younger. But self-control and discipline are supernatural gifts. Look at

> God gave us a spirit not of fear but of power and love and self-control.
>
> —2 Timothy 1:7

Jesus: he lived his life as the only perfect young man ever to walk the planet. He was at times filled with righteous anger. He wept. He sharply rebuked those who deserved it. He had close friends and associates who could be incredibly irritating. And he never lost control, ever. Jesus gives us his ability for self-control through the Holy Spirit.

Self-control over destructive expressions of emotion is so important—and it's something that we men often struggle to master. Angry hearts spew out angry words and angry words wreck people we care about. Understanding the truth that God the Father loves us as sons and carefully orders all that we experience throws cold water on angry and hot hearts. We'll talk about self-control in the realm of sexuality, too, in chapter 8.

So What Now?

I still recall vividly a high school football game I played in during my senior year. It was the game I pretty much lost for my team. Worse yet, it was against one of our staunchest rivals. My errors were so bad that I made the local newspaper. Although the coach didn't use my name, he revealed me by position and suggested that my mistakes cost us the game. He was right in his assessment, as I think back on it. But strangely, I have no regrets or shame about that game.

I played in the secondary on the defensive side of the ball. And I made some great plays that night in addition to a couple of bad plays at critical times. I remember playing fearlessly. Here's why: my dad was at every game, and no matter how I performed, he always would support me. I played with nothing to prove and nothing to lose. After each game, we would review what had gone well and what had gone wrong, but he always was loving. A son who knows he is loved by his dad is free to succeed big or fail big. He is loved.

I hurt for you, even if I haven't met you, if you have grown up without a loving earthly father. I am so sorry. But please know your life isn't ruined because your dad wasn't there—or if he *was* there and you wished he weren't. As a Christian, you are a beloved son of the Father. And he loves you with all the love he has for his Son, Jesus.

There's one more benefit to being a son of our heavenly Father. Even if your earthly father is absent, either emotionally or physically, you still can have a spiritual father. You can find a mentor and father just like fatherless Timothy found in sonless Paul. Jesus has given you his church to be your family. The church isn't an event or a place. The church is a people. As a dear son of the Father, when you find your place in this spiritual family (we'll talk more about that in chapter 7), I am confident Jesus will give you spiritual dads to fill in the gap. Ask a more mature and trustworthy man to help you grow as a man who thinks, feels, speaks, and acts like Jesus. Someone will find joy in guiding you in the faith just as Paul found joy in Timothy, and as I have, many times, in receiving a spiritual son into the family.

Finally, since you are perfectly loved by the Father, spend your strength in helping other sons and daughters find the love of the Father. Ask the Holy Spirit to fill you with the Father's love (see Galatians 4:6). Then let the Father's love pour out of you into the lives of others.

3

—

BROTHER

December 2006

Dear Son,

It has been a rough month of school for your sister
Jillian. One of her male classmates angrily called her
a bitch in front of her friends in class. She wasn't quite
sure what to do, but she felt that she needed to let
someone in authority know she didn't feel safe. She
first went to her teacher, who sent her on to a guidance
counselor. The guidance counselor suggested Jillian
directly confront the young man. Needless to say, this
didn't make her feel any safer. The young man who
insulted her was untrustworthy.

So Jillian decided to move on and let it go. I told
her if he did or said anything else disrespectful, he
and I would have a "man to little man" talk. Within
weeks, the same young man was taken into custody
for bringing a loaded handgun to school. This incident

43

made Jillian feel confident that she had done the wise thing by avoiding a direct confrontation. And she also learned the painful lesson that not everyone has good intentions toward her. Not every girl in her school would treat her as a beloved sister. And not every boy would value her as a brother should.

Rather than be angry with the young man who had threatened his classmates, I felt pity for him. It was rumored that his stepfather, with whom he lived at the time, was a gang member. Jillian's classmate was probably just reenacting what he watched happen at home. Shortly after his stepson's arrest for the illegal possession of a firearm, the suspected gangster stepdad died from a drug overdose. More lives were ruined. More families were torn apart. More cycles of heartbreak were spun into motion.

David, the world needs more young men who treat others, especially women, as family members: with kindness and respect. We need more caring brothers and fewer careless boys. Son, what kind of brother would you have been?

For Jesus' fame,
Dad

■ ■ ■

The last days of December 2006 were some of the darkest of my life. I was pastoring a small church in Albuquerque, New

Mexico. Shericka Hill, a young woman just nineteen years old and an active participant in our church for several years, was brutally murdered by a man who was paying her to dance for him in his trailer home. Shericka's "boyfriend," Frederick Williams, dropped her off to perform the private dance for a man named Lorenzo Montoya in exchange for five hundred dollars. According to police reports, as Frederick waited in his car for Shericka to finish her dance, Lorenzo suddenly came out of his home with Shericka's lifeless, nude body in his arms. He had strangled her with a noose made from duct tape and shoelaces.

Frederick walked up to Lorenzo and shot him to death.

A few short days later, I was peering into Shericka's lifeless face as she lay in her open casket. I was racked with shock, grief, and the shame that comes when you feel as if you've failed someone terribly and tragically. I had failed in a way that resulted in something more than hardship in life. I had failed in a way that ended a life altogether. I tried not to stare at her or linger too long at her casket, but I couldn't quite pull myself away.

My daughters loved Shericka. They didn't know her as a close friend, but like everyone else, they were drawn to Shericka's kindness and beauty. Once when we were coming home from a youth group trip to Six Flags, my girls shared the twelve-hour drive with Shericka; her little sister, Sherelle; and her friend Lilly. Shericka had taken the time and care, as an amateur beautician, to fix each of the girls' hair into tight and neatly arranged cornrows. They had the time of their lives. They never would have said as much, but it was a dream come true to have their hair done by someone as hip and beautiful as Shericka. They now were officially cool among their youth group peers. Even more important, they felt very loved by this older girl.

Yet at Shericka's funeral, they each stood with a sense of shocking loss as they, too, looked into the casket at her face. Although they had heard about death, they never had seen it face-to-face like this in their young lives. (When we lost David, Lisa was only sixteen months old, and the other girls hadn't been born yet.) Unlike me, they moved quickly after glancing into Shericka's casket. It seemed they felt as if they were looking at something they never should have to see. I wonder if Jesus didn't feel the same way. Lisa, Lauren, Jennifer, and Jillian wouldn't talk about their experience of seeing Shericka in her casket for months. But then, sometime later, we talked about it almost daily. It was a very tough time for all of us.

I remember standing up at the funeral to speak to the mourners and preaching the words of Jesus from John 14:1-3: "Let not your hearts be troubled. Believe in God; believe also in me. In my Father's house are many rooms. If it were not so, would I have told you that I go to prepare a place for you? And if I go and prepare a place for you, I will come again and will take you to myself, that where I am you may be also."

I have led many funerals in my life as a pastor. More than a few have been for younger people. I haven't before or since spoken to a more hurting and hopeless group of people than those at Shericka's funeral. From some of the younger men present I felt a steely, coldhearted hatred. Not so much toward me personally but more toward a world they fight against every day—winning some battles along the way but knowing deep down inside the war is being lost. Frederick, Shericka's "boyfriend," executed a fellow member of his "Memphis Mob" a few months later and will spend much, if not the rest, of his life in prison.

After I got home that night, I couldn't sleep. My sense of failing Shericka morphed from heartbreak to resolve in the weeks that followed. I started to see the problem more clearly than ever before. Clarity, although at times very painful, is a powerful thing. What had taken Shericka's life was killing my city, too. Men were the demise of Shericka Hill. Her dad failed her. Her boyfriend used her for money. Her client used her for sex, strangled her, then discarded her like a cheap disposable razor. Although technically only one young man killed Shericka, many more young men were responsible for her hard life. Her story—perhaps not as dramatic but basically the same—was playing out all around me every day. Although I am sure I made some difference in Shericka's life, that difference wasn't enough. Maybe what she needed, in the absence of her father, was a brother. A young man who refused to abuse or use her, but who instead chose to protect her purity. Hope for our cities, countries, and world lies in the hearts of young men loving and serving women and children instead of using and abusing them. Jesus alone is able to change and redirect angry and broken hordes of young men.

We live in a brutal world. Sadly, much of its violence is directed toward women. I want for you what I would have wanted for my son: that you be a man of courage and a good brother and friend to the women in your life. In a culture that devalues women, I want you to fight for purity in how you love and protect your mother, your sisters, and your friends. I am quite sure this is exactly what the apostle Paul had in mind when he penned these words to Pastor Timothy, his spiritual son: "Do not rebuke an older man but encourage him as you would a father, younger men as brothers, older women as mothers, *younger women as sisters, in all purity*" (1 Timothy 5:1-2, emphasis added). Women in the early church were vulnerable to false teachers who came to town and lured them into harmful sexual relationships (Paul alludes to this in 2 Timothy 3:6-7). That sounds exactly like the culture we live in today. Men use a false faith to get close to women so they can use them sexually.

While Pastor Timothy, as a shepherd of God's flock, perhaps had more responsibility than other young Christian men around him, there is much in these verses to be applied for all young men. If we condense this text, the charge is to "encourage younger women as sisters, in all purity." If I have learned something in raising daughters over the past two and a half decades, it's that young women need young men to encourage them and treat them with purity.

The Greek word translated "encourage" could also be translated "plead." The idea is that danger or opportunity is ahead and a good and wise decision must be made. *Encourage* means to make a personal plea to choose wisely in light of the consequences. *To encourage* can also mean "to comfort." Being present as a source of strength for young women as they walk through life's storms is important too. Women need to be reminded they are far more than sex objects or status symbols who exist for the pleasure of men. They are created in the image of God to mirror his greatness. Women exist for God just as men do. They have intrinsic dignity.

Shericka needed encouragement. She desperately needed to know that her life and destiny were endangered. Perhaps she received encouragement

> *Encourage . . .*
> *younger women as*
> *sisters, in all purity.*
> —1 Timothy 5:1-2

from a brother and ignored the warning. But if so, no one ever mentioned that to me. It would seem that the men in her life led her toward death rather than turn her away from it.

Many women are deeply rooted in false identities based on sexual attraction and body image. In our culture, women are ruthlessly barraged by lies. A woman is told that her height, weight, waistline, bust size, wardrobe, and personality—as judged by men—define her identity. I have counseled far too many young women who live in a prison of loneliness and despair because they have yielded to cultural distortions about what it means to be women.

To make matters even worse, this is an unjust world where men regularly get away with abusing women emotionally, sexually, and physically. Young women desperately need encouragement. Someone with strength and credibility—someone they will listen to and trust—must plead with young women and warn them of lurking dangers.

Donald is a strong young man who is growing in yielding to Jesus. And as he does, he has found the opportunity to serve, rather than use, young women. Donald, a star athlete, used to take advantage of women for his own selfish purposes, with little or no concern about the consequences those women surely would face. Now he serves the young women he knows by encouraging them to know Jesus. He recently helped Laura understand that she, too, is loved by Jesus in a way that frees her from having to chase after men who don't love her. She is experiencing liberation. She no longer fears that she never will be loved. And she is strong and stable instead of being needy and vulnerable.

You can be that kind of encourager best when you see women as sisters, not as potential romantic partners or even as friends. While friendship isn't intrinsically wrong, it certainly involves less than the bond of loyalty and care that exists between a brother and sister. Friends come and go; family is forever. Casual and passing friendships between young men and young women often lack definition and purpose. Perhaps they are fun, but most often they are fleeting and sometimes confusing to one or both participants. Too many times these friendships end with someone getting hurt. I have watched my daughters time and time again naively assume the best of men who approach them as "just friends" but who actually are looking for something more. Once an immature young man's romantic hopes are disappointed, he angrily and awkwardly walks away from the friendship. The woman on the receiving end of this foolishness is hurt and wounded.

While Christian men should be friendly to everyone, including Christian women, we must have a deeper commitment than friendship to these women. We must see ourselves as responsible and protective brothers who serve our sisters. One of the greatest gifts God gives to us in Jesus is a big family known as the church. This means that we are to relate to other members of God's family much as we would relate to members of our biological family. We must be committed, through the power of the Holy Spirit, to see our sisters grow into women who think, feel, speak, and act like Jesus: in all purity.

The great risk to Christian young men and Christian young women in viewing so many others as potential spouses is that purity may be compromised. The end

We must see ourselves as responsible and protective brothers who serve our sisters.

result of carelessness in this regard is that many young Christians enter into marriage having already given themselves emotionally and sexually to someone other than their spouse. The biblical idea isn't to try on potential spouses like shirts and pants while shopping at the mall. As a matter of fact, the subject of dating is never addressed in the Bible. Biblically, the idea is to pursue one person for life with the wise counsel and input from spiritually qualified members of our church family. (We'll talk more about this in chapter 8.) One of the greatest preventive and proactive ways to achieve this pursuit is to view all young and single Christian women as "sisters, in all purity."

A sister is worthy of your respect. A sister is worthy of your protection. A sister's highest calling is living purely in the power of the Holy Spirit. So if you really love your sisters in Jesus Christ, you will respect them by responsibly protecting their purity. You will encourage them to avoid purity pitfalls. You never will see them as sex objects or status symbols in the way our society does. You regularly will encourage them about who they really are: beloved and righteous daughters of our loving Father.

Our culture chews up and spits out women like baseball players in the dugout devour sunflower seeds and spit out the hulls. But women have high value in the sight of God. The sons of God in Jesus are charged by him to love, serve, and protect the daughters of God in Jesus just as a brother does his sister.

It's not only young Christian women who need brothers; so do young Christian men. Shericka needed a brother, but so did Frederick. It's obvious that his fellow gang members didn't help him make something productive of his life. Maybe he was looking for something in a gang that he could have found in Jesus and his family. One of the reasons gangs are so attractive to young men is that they offer a form of brotherhood, even if it's severely distorted. I've met many young men who pursue the same path as Frederick because they feel alone, vulnerable, and in need of protection. Others have told me they joined up just to scratch the itch of boredom.

They wanted and needed a band of brothers. They wanted to achieve something. They wanted to conquer someone.

No band of brothers ever has had a more worthy cause to fight for than young men owning the Great Commission and proclaiming the Kingdom of Jesus. His Kingdom is eternal. His Kingdom is righteous and good. His Kingdom never retreats. But like every other kingdom that has advanced in the history of the world, Christ's Kingdom faces resistance and warfare, and these bring about the certainty of fatigue, disillusionment, and discouragement. So brothers at war need other brothers at war for protection, direction, and encouragement.

You will need Christian men to stick closer to you than the friends you make in class or at the gym or in the office. You will need brothers from church, your larger family, if you are going to fight the good fight for King Jesus. And they will need you. You must plead with them, much as you do with your sisters, to be loyal to King Jesus.

There are many distractions in this world that can hurt a brother. Young men in particular are susceptible to the three categories of worldliness listed in 1 John 2:15-17: pleasures, possessions, and pride.

God has created us to experience *pleasure* as an act of worship toward him. We find pleasure in food, drink, sex, and sleep. When we find pleasure in these good things in a God-centered way, we worship God. But when pleasure becomes an end in itself rather than the means to worship, we become idolaters.

Matt enjoyed a beer in the pub with his friends after work.

He even talked about the Bible and Jesus with his friends while they unwound from a busy day. This was a simple pleasure. But Matt would go home after his friends left and drink himself into a stupor. He was an alcoholic. What was meant to be a gift became Matt's god. And the god of drink was cruel, unforgiving, and enslaving.

Plead with your brothers to put pleasure in the proper perspective. Pleasure can be a good thing, but it never should be a god thing. When pleasure becomes a god thing, it is addictive and destructive. Pleasure is the cruelest idol of all. It never fully satisfies but always teases its worshiper with more until he is destroyed.

A second source of distraction is *possessions*. Material things are not evil in themselves. Our belongings can provide opportunities to worship Jesus and serve people. But when Jesus becomes a currency by which to stockpile houses, cars, tech gadgets, and other things, then everything is inside out and upside down. Some men see Jesus only as the Giver rather than as the greatest Gift. And so they try to manipulate and use the Giver to obtain as many good gifts as possible. But the man who understands that Jesus is the real Gift enjoys his other gifts in a secondary way.

Possessions have a worldly way of taking hold of their possessor. Be careful. Be a man who loves his brothers enough to plead and warn them of the pending danger in building their lives around stuff. Jesus said that his followers have no right to claim ownership of their possessions. All of their stuff belongs to him. He states in Luke 14:33, "Any one of you who does not renounce all that he has cannot be my disciple." This means that a true follower of Jesus signs the title of all he may possess over to Jesus. Then he lives life as Jesus' agent, using what were formerly his possessions in the manner that Jesus chooses.

Dan is a good example of that. He works hard but doesn't make much money yet. He does cover his costs and is able to save a little bit each month so that someday he can buy a home for himself and his future wife. She hasn't shown up yet, as far as we know. Dan also sets aside money so that he can take Steve out for a nice dinner once a month. Steve has a mental illness and lives in a group home. He pays for the cost of his care from his disability check and has very little left over—certainly not enough to enjoy a good meal once a month without Dan's generosity. But Dan gets the fact that the money in his account actually belongs to Jesus. And Jesus wants him to buy Steve dinner so that Steve will know Jesus cares for him, too.

A third source of distraction is *pride*. Unlike with possessions, there is nothing good at all about pride. Pride is looking at life through the lens of our performance and achievement. Pride offends God like nothing else. Everything good we are and every good thing we do ultimately are achieved by Jesus. Humbly knowing this is incredibly liberating. Plead with your brothers to rid themselves of pride. The easiest way to do this is simply ask the question why. *Why* gets at the motive of the heart, where pride makes its home. *Why did you do that? Why did you say that? Why do you feel that way?* You don't have to function as a pride policeman. It's best to let the person you suspect of pride find it rotting in his own heart like mold. It's the most destructive sin living in the heart of the young Christian man. It may be dormant for a season, but when it comes alive, it always kills joy.

You and I need to be good brothers, by God's grace, to our sisters and brothers in Jesus' family. A good brother is loyal and helpful. Most of all, he takes responsibility for his spiritual siblings. I believe it takes a brother to make a brother. Someday soon you will desperately need help from your brothers and sisters in Jesus. Stay close to them. Stay connected to them. Serve them and be served by them. It's the way God has made his family so that we grow together in Jesus. If you live as a brother, you will be stronger—and so will your family of faith.

So What Now?

Maybe you're realizing you haven't been much of a brother to anyone. Or maybe you've been a bad brother to everyone. Or perhaps you just want to be a better brother. What can you do next?

First, invite the Holy Spirit to search your life for sin. Ask him if you have wronged anyone as a brother. Second, as the Spirit reveals your sin to you, agree with his findings. Find forgiveness in the death of Jesus for your sake and your sin. Ask the Holy Spirit for his help in making you a better brother. If he brings people to mind that you have hurt, take the initiative and go seek their forgiveness. Humbly and sincerely let them know you are sorry you have failed them. Finally, ask the Holy Spirit to make you keenly aware of those within your sphere of influence whom you can love and serve like a good brother. As he brings people for you to serve, be the brother that Jesus has made you to be.

4

YOUNG MAN

Dear Son,

Recently, your sister Jenn graduated from high school.
As with so many life events, I wished you could have
been with us. It's these kinds of occasions—when the
whole family is gathered together for big events—that
we miss you most. Your absence is like an open and
bleeding wound that can't be sutured shut. We survive
without you, but we are hurting and weak from the pain
of losing you.

Had you been there with us, I know you would
have been so proud of your little sister Jenn. After her
sophomore year, she transferred from Sandia High
School in Albuquerque, where she was thriving, to
Roosevelt High School in Seattle. Her junior and senior
years were very trying. She left many great friends
behind and found very few new friends. But she not

only overcame social challenges, she also overcame having to start all over again academically. Her new school didn't recognize the honors classes she took in Albuquerque and the accompanying higher grade point average. So she slid down the ladder of standing in her new class. But she made great grades, was accepted at all the universities she applied to, and will be receiving a solid scholarship to attend the college she chose as her favorite.

The graduation ceremony was rather interesting and controversial, particularly the commencement speech. It was delivered by one of Roosevelt's most famous alums, award-winning author David Guterson. He went ten minutes beyond his allotted fifteen-minute time slot. But that isn't so unusual for these types of events. What was unexpected was the subject of his talk. Guterson talked mostly about death being inescapable and happiness in life being mostly elusive.

It was totally Solomonic, right out of the pages of the Old Testament book of Ecclesiastes: "I have seen everything that is done under the sun, and behold, all is vanity and a striving after wind" (Ecclesiastes 1:14). It was the perfect setup for the gospel. But rather than crushing a home run over the center-field wall, Guterson fouled out by missing the gospel. He clipped the part of the ball that points to needing Jesus while missing the core, which is all about Jesus. All in all, it was a very smart but very empty talk.

At one point during his speech, with the graduates' families and friends in the stands of Memorial Stadium growing restless and uncomfortable, a young man from Jenn's class stood up in his green graduation cap and gown and tried to shout Guterson down. It was vintage Seattle. It was also a typical young-man response. I looked around to see most of the adults sitting by me roll their eyes or shake their heads in disapproval at this young man. He was largely dismissed while Guterson continued with his dark and depressing speech. And that was a common response to a young man's passionate words: complete dismissal.

Son, I believe that young men have valuable contributions to make to the world. And I think they should be heard. Sadly, most young men don't understand how to get their serious ideas taken seriously. I love to think you would have been different. I like to believe that you would have been a young man people paid attention to and that you would have brought some good to this world that is desperately in need of help. I am proud of you, who you are, and who I think you might have been. I love you!

For Jesus' fame,

Dad

. . .

Jenn's bold but dismissed classmate illustrates one of the greatest obstacles a young man faces in life. You may wish to help an older friend or family member with counsel that, if taken, could make a positive difference. Yet your wisdom is ignored. Or maybe you have a great, creative idea that could help your school, your company, or your church be more effective. But no one who is in a position to implement your idea is listening to you. You easily are dismissed, mostly because you lack experience and credibility. Experience can be gained only through years of success and failure. So what can a young man do to overcome the prejudice of his older peers in life? How can you avoid being dismissed by others?

I have to admit, we live in a world where a lot of young men really are shortsighted, foolish, and often wasteful. At the same time, there is something good and noble about the grit and determination and idealism that seem to come with being young. But the track record of most men in our culture today isn't impressive, and the good men often are lumped in with the boys and easily are dismissed.

The sonless apostle Paul gives fatherless Pastor Timothy counsel on this very issue in 1 Timothy 4:12. As Timothy leads men and women many years his senior, he receives this inspired instruction from his mentor: "Let no one despise you for your youth, but set the believers an example in speech, in conduct, in love, in faith, in purity."

While there are timeless cultural similarities between

first-century Ephesus and modern-day America, one difference must be understood in order to frame this passage accurately. In the ancient Roman world, older people were much
more highly esteemed than they are in our world today. The
term translated "youth" in this passage most likely meant

or Timothy wasn't a
college making his
He was most likely in
g men in our world
egarded as an idealist
helpful wisdom that
e.
and understands the
ke Timothy seriously.
o work on to provide
ve a positive influence
to set an example for
a young man. I don't
otential influence for
have been shaving for
iously means you must
hers in the things you
say and do.

I believe you have much to offer anyone and everyone
who watches you and listens to you, if—and only if—you
live out your faith in front of them. We all need real-life
examples within our reach of what it looks like to follow Jesus

in faith throughout the many stages of life. We need boys, girls, youth, young men, young women, singles, marrieds, old men, and old women to walk out their faith in Jesus. We need real-life walking and talking examples of people just like us who love Jesus. As we watch them, we can be encouraged to follow their example.

From my limited experience I have observed that young men most often seem to miss out on this opportunity to impact others. Test me on this. Count how many young men you know personally who are worthy of emulation. You probably could count them on a single hand that has survived some serious shop-class mishaps. Exemplary young men who love Jesus and serve others selflessly don't come around often.

Paul gives us two mediums of influence by which young men can make Jesus known. Timothy is to set an example first in the sphere of his speech, and second in the area of his conduct. Said differently, young Timothy can capture the attention of those around him through his words and his actions.

While very few young men are called to be preachers in the church, every young man preaches both to himself and to those who listen to his words.

Timothy spoke many words as a pastor responsible for preaching and teaching in the church. If you're not a preacher, it would be easy to discount the potential impact of your words for good. But this would be an enormous mistake. While very few first-century Ephesus and modern-day America, one difference must be understood in order to frame this passage accurately. In the ancient Roman world, older people were much more highly esteemed than they are in our world today. The term translated "youth" in this passage most likely meant anyone under forty years of age. Pastor Timothy wasn't a twenty-two-year-old graduate of Bible college making his way in life with his first serious job. He was most likely in his thirties. Yet very much like young men in our world today, Timothy quickly could be disregarded as an idealist rather than an experienced man with the helpful wisdom that comes from firsthand knowledge of life.

Paul is all too familiar with culture and understands the propensity for older people not to take Timothy seriously. So Paul gives Timothy some things to work on to provide the credibility he needs in order to have a positive influence among those he is serving: Timothy is to set an example for others to follow.

I want you to be taken seriously as a young man. I don't want anyone to miss out on your potential influence for good and for God just because you have been shaving for less than a decade. But to be taken seriously means you must have something of worth to offer others in the things you say and do.

I believe you have much to offer anyone and everyone who watches you and listens to you, if—and only if—you live out your faith in front of them. We all need real-life examples within our reach of what it looks like to follow Jesus in faith throughout the many stages of life. We need boys, girls, youth, young men, young women, singles, marrieds, old men, and old women to walk out their faith in Jesus. We need real-life walking and talking examples of people just like us who love Jesus. As we watch them, we can be encouraged to follow their example.

From my limited experience I have observed that young men most often seem to miss out on this opportunity to impact others. Test me on this. Count how many young men you know personally who are worthy of emulation. You probably could count them on a single hand that has survived some serious shop-class mishaps. Exemplary young men who love Jesus and serve others selflessly don't come around often.

Paul gives us two mediums of influence by which young men can make Jesus known. Timothy is to set an example first in the sphere of his speech, and second in the area of his conduct. Said differently, young Timothy can capture the attention of those around him through his words and his actions.

While very few young men are called to be preachers in the church, every young man preaches both to himself and to those who listen to his words.

Timothy spoke many words as a pastor responsible for preaching and teaching in the church. If you're not a preacher, it would be easy to discount the potential impact of your words for good. But this would be an enormous mistake. While very few young men are called to be preachers in the church, every young man preaches both to himself and to those who listen to his words.

Your words matter a lot. They are powerful and can have a great impact on others. As a twentysomething pastor a couple of decades ago, I learned the hard way that my words are powerful. When I spoke carelessly and critically or tried to comfort my own insecurities by receiving laughs through adolescent humor, my words hurt my chances to help others. But when I spoke what was true and did so out of love and care for others, my words changed lives. Ideas are very powerful. And the words that express ideas make a difference. They always have. It doesn't matter whether you are two years old or twenty-two years old. You're always preaching, whether you stand in the pulpit before hundreds of congregants or at the watercooler before a handful of colleagues. So you must make your words count, because the people listening count in the eyes and heart of God.

But here's the deal with mastering our words so others benefit: we can't control our words by working on our oratory skills, because words aren't governed by the mouth. The brain doesn't determine them either. According to Jesus, words come from the heart. He said it this way: "What comes out of the mouth proceeds from the heart" (Matthew 15:18). So the key to changing our words for the better is experiencing a change of heart. This is exactly the realm in which Jesus does his very best work.

If we want our speech to be filled with words about Jesus,

our hearts must first be flooded with affection for him. This can happen only as we offer our hearts to Jesus as a place to make his home. Colossians 3:16 reads, "Let the word of Christ dwell in you richly, teaching and admonishing one another in all wisdom, singing psalms and hymns and spiritual songs, with thankfulness in your hearts to God." A similar passage, Ephesians 5:18-19, states, "Do not get drunk with wine, for that is debauchery, but be filled with the Spirit, addressing one another in psalms and hymns and spiritual songs, singing and making melody to the Lord with your heart."

Do you see the progression? Our hearts are changed by believing in Jesus' gospel (the "Word of Christ"), and then the Holy Spirit controls us so that our hearts are so flooded with thankfulness and joy that they spill over in words about Jesus to others. The best thing we can do to have helpful words for others is to have hearts ruled by Jesus. When our hearts are filled with love and worship for Jesus, our words will overflow from our hearts, through our mouths, and into the ears of listeners. We talk most about the things and people we love best. And nothing is more helpful or timely to those we deeply care about than words describing Jesus.

When I first met Brian, he was a young man who was confused about Jesus. He believed Jesus existed, but he wasn't quite sure what else to believe about him. Consequently, his words confused most people. Other people, especially his friends and peers, dismissed him as a young guy who was still trying to figure out just what he believed. But Brian began to learn about the real Jesus from the Bible. I remember him lingering after church services to ask me questions—good questions and hard questions. And he listened carefully to the answers. He studied the Bible diligently. He was teachable. He was hungry to know the real Jesus. And as he came to know the real Jesus, he also worshiped him. A few years later, Brian was paid the highest compliment by an older couple who were thinking about leaving the church. They chose to stay because they were so impressed by the example that young Brian set with his speech.

The very same formula that applies to words holds true for our conduct and actions. Again Jesus, in the very same passage in which he connects words to the heart, states, "Out of the heart come evil thoughts, murder, adultery, sexual immorality, theft, false witness, slander" (Matthew 15:19). Bad words and bad works come from bad hearts. This is why Paul connects love, faith, and purity to being an example in word and action.

Let no one despise you for your youth, but set the believers an example in speech, in conduct, in love, in faith, in purity.
—1 Timothy 4:12

A heart that is filled with *love*, the very love that comes to us from God in Jesus through the Holy Spirit, is one that produces good words and good works. The big idea with this concept is that the love we now hold in our hearts flows first from God, then into our hearts, and then out into the lives of other Christians. In this way, a man without much life experience still can be a great example of love for others to follow. Take Jacob, for example. He is still in his twenties. He has had a hard life as a cancer survivor. And while he doesn't have a big résumé, he has a big heart. He loves his wife well. He loves his church well. He loves beyond his years. And Jacob is taken seriously by all who know him, young and old, because love doesn't come intrinsically based on our experience or environment. It comes to us from God through Jesus as a free gift to be received and passed on by faith.

You also can be a good role model for others to follow in expressing words and initiating actions grounded in *faith*. Faith most simply means to believe or trust. Some words are best understood by considering their opposites. I believe this is the case with the biblical idea of faith. The opposite of faith most often is thought of as doubt or disbelief. But surprisingly, in the Bible, the opposite of faith is works. Faith is as valuable as the object of its trust. The object of biblical faith is Jesus. Faith is about trusting in him entirely for forgiveness from the penalty of sin. It's about trusting in him entirely for freedom from the power of sin. But the object of works, as it is depicted negatively in the Bible, is you, not Jesus. Faith trusts in Jesus alone to bring about the needed change. Works tries harder to make change happen through self-effort and self-righteousness.

In this sense, being an example of faith as expressed in words and actions is trusting completely in Jesus for the needed heart change that is foundational for helpful words and actions. Men of faith talk openly about their wrongs, their sin. Men of works talk about just that: what they are working on in order to be acceptable to God. As always, words reveal the heart from which they flow. And a heart of faith talks about repentance: turning from specific sin and trusting in Jesus to forgive and free. But a heart of works talks about religious achievements: boasting about personal actions rather than about what Jesus has done.

You don't have to be older to have a great faith. Remember, the quality of your faith is based entirely on the value of its object. You can have an impactful faith because it rests entirely on Jesus. He empowers your words and actions through his gospel and the Holy Spirit. When others see a young man trusting completely in Jesus for forgiveness of sin and the freedom to live for him, they most certainly will be challenged. As they are challenged, they might even be changed by Jesus, who specializes in transforming hearts.

Finally, Jesus desires you to live in and live out the *purity* only he can give. To be pure most basically means to be free of contamination, or untainted. It is a condition of the deepest sort, one that exists at the level of motive. So once again, purity isn't gained through years of experience. You don't need to have much experience to have much purity. In fact, purity potentially is compromised with age and time. While this reality should serve as a warning to all, it also should encourage men who are lacking in life experience. Through the finished work of Jesus applied by the Holy Spirit to the very heart of who you are, you can be a man whose words and works are exemplary, grounded in a pure faith and a pure love.

Another area that falls under pure conduct is very important to flee. Paul warns Timothy to run away from youthful lusts. He says, "Flee youthful passions and pursue righteousness, faith, love, and peace, along with those who call on the Lord from a pure heart" (2 Timothy 2:22). While this verse often is considered to refer to sexual lust, limiting the text to that meaning alone is restrictive. While sexual lust is wrong, you can have other lustful desires that are wrong too. You can desire fortune, fame, or power in the most destructive ways.

"Youthful passions" are the desires for things apart from Jesus that are most common for younger people. It can mean desire for sex outside of marriage. But it also can mean an unhealthy craving for food or drink. This phrase could also include the idea of immature and ungodly ambition, a passion for fame and success.

It's the last category that I see taking so many young men captive. Young men usually are idealistic and ambitious. Some men are out to do more than change the world—they are out to conquer it. In other words, instead of using their strength to make the world a better place for others, they waste it trying to make the world a better place only for themselves. This is a futile thing to attempt, because King Jesus already has conquered the world. It all belongs to him. It all is for him. And all that is left to do is to proclaim his Kingdom on earth as it is in heaven. Why would you try to conquer something that Jesus has taken already? Especially since Jesus wants you to enjoy his Kingdom as you worship him.

So much time and energy are wasted in the pursuit of things that leave us empty and unfulfilled. Sex without marital, emotional, and spiritual intimacy. Aiming to achieve celebrity for self apart from Jesus' fame. Temporal and earthly treasure gained at the forfeiture of riches that are eternal and heavenly. All these examples fall into the category of "youthful passions." So Paul sternly warns young Timothy—and young men like you—to run from these passions. Escape from them as you would from a house on fire. Don't worry about what might burn in the fire. Just be sure *you* don't.

Paul does more than tell Timothy and other young men like you what to run *from*; he tells them *where* to run. This is one of the most important lessons a man can embrace. You are always running. The pressing issue is, from where and to where are you running?

The opposite of fleeing something is pursuing something. We consistently should be *fleeing from* one thing and *running toward* another. This is the biblical concept of repentance. Young men should run away from "youthful passions" so they may run toward "righteousness, faith, love, and peace" (2 Timothy 2:22). All of these traits belong to Jesus. He makes them come alive in us by faith. Said differently, we are to turn away from the sinful desires that tempt us and run toward Jesus, while trusting him to satisfy us with what he alone can give.

So What Now?

One fascinating thing about this passage of Scripture is what it reveals about the race we are running: it isn't an individual event but a team relay. We are to run "along with those who call on the Lord from a pure heart" (2 Timothy 2:22). Sin is contagious among Christians. So are purity and faith. Whom you choose to run with largely will determine what you believe and how you live. I will never be able to stress enough the importance of being a member of a local church that takes pursuing Jesus and running toward him seriously. If you wish to live as a man who is helpful to others, a model that encourages and an example to follow, you must always be running from sin and running toward Jesus. You must be running with others who are doing the same.

Here are two very important and practical things you can do to be taken seriously by others because you live a life worth copying. First, practice self-examination. Spend time at the end of every day asking the Holy Spirit to show you where you aren't a man who is thinking, feeling, speaking, or acting like Jesus. Be quiet and listen. The Spirit will direct you to an area of your life where change is needed. He may guide you to a Bible passage to consider. He may lead you by some other means. But you can be certain that if you ask him for input, he most certainly will give it. The key to true and consistent heart change is to tackle it as a daily and persistent project.

Second, practice confession with other Christians. The Bible has this to say about being open with others about your sin: "*Confess your sins to one another* and pray for one another, that you may be healed. The prayer of a righteous person has great power as it is working" (James 5:16, emphasis added). Pray with others who want to be changed as you do. Having extra sets of eyes looking into your life and searching for blind spots is critical to inside-out, from-the-heart-to-the-mouth-to-the-lives-of-others faith. As your heart changes, so will your words and your actions. And so will your impact on the lives of others.

Don't be dismissed because you are young. Instead, speak and act in a way that comes from a heart that loves people and trusts Jesus. Live this way, and you will make an enormous impact, even as a young man. It doesn't matter how many people are watching. What matters is that you understand *someone* is. You can have big influence. You are an example to someone. You have something valuable to offer all people. You belong to Jesus. You can be an example of his grace and glory. Trust him to live in you and through you as you are honest about your sin and selfishness. And as you grow, you will learn that your example will be hard to ignore. You will lead the kind of life that can't be dismissed by anyone. Your impact will be big, and people will take notice of how Jesus is working in you.

5

PROVIDER

Dear Son,

Your sister Lauren had a big day recently. I drove her
to the ferry so she could make it to Bainbridge Island
to begin her internship for a start-up coffee retailer.
I was shocked at how grown-up she looked decked
out in her business attire. She's worked really hard
at her studies and will graduate with a bachelor's
degree in retail management in only three years.
She was nervous and excited all at the same time.
I marveled at how quickly time had passed since she
was a little girl. It seemed that it was only yesterday
when she spent the entire day wearing her *Lion King*
one-piece swimsuit and singing Disney princess
songs. Today she was a grown woman ready to take
on the world. She was beginning what might become
a career.

I also heard some apprehension in her voice when we prayed together before she headed off to work. Her biggest goal isn't to have a successful business career. Her deepest desire is to be a wife and then a mom. According to Scripture, this is the very thing God wants for her too: "Train the young women to love their husbands and children, to be self-controlled, pure, working at home, kind, and submissive to their own husbands, that the word of God may not be reviled" (Titus 2:4-5).

I have watched many young women linger in this type of apprehension. It's not long until apprehension becomes fear and fear turns to regret. Some young women who, unlike Lauren, are already married and have kids, deeply regret having to work hard outside the home to pay the bills. They would love to be able to devote themselves fully to raising their kids. They have outside work not because they want to but because they have to—mostly because their husbands aren't able to earn enough money to provide for their families in a way that allows their wives, the mothers of their children, to be homeward focused full-time. There is much more here to explore than a progressive culture and changing values. This scenario has less to do with feminism and equality in the church community and far more to do with the huge failure of Christian men to see how important it is to God that they provide financially for their families, and that they do so in a way that allows for Mom to be home with her children as a full-time venture.

David, when I held you in my arms for the first time, I loved you so much! I would have wanted your mom to stay with you as often as possible until you one day left our home as an adult. She is a wonderful, nurturing, and available mom to your sisters. I desperately need her help as I lead our home. I'm grateful to be on a path that allows me to provide for our family so your mom has been free to stay at home and care for your sisters full-time. Any sacrifices I've had to make have been more than worth it. Son, as a matter of fact, providing financially for my family has been one of the greatest thrills of my life. If you were here today, I would want you to know this same happiness. As always, I dream about who you would have been, and I love you.

For Jesus' fame,

Dad

. . .

How important is providing for your family? The apostle Paul writes a verse to young Timothy that should terrify all men: "If anyone does not provide for his relatives, and especially for members of his household, he has denied the faith and is worse than an unbeliever" (1 Timothy 5:8). It is very difficult to imagine a fate worse than that of an unbeliever. He will spend eternity in torment under the wrath of God. Yet the

Bible has a more tragic category: a man who doesn't provide for his family is considered to be worse than an unbeliever.

The only way you can be saved is through faith in Jesus alone, by grace alone, to the glory of God alone. You can't save yourself. Nor are there multiple options or menus to choose from in order to be saved. Jesus alone saves all sinners, including you.

But there are many ways you can deny having the faith that will save you. This scary verse doesn't mean that you intellectually deny the propositions of biblical faith. It means instead that you practically deny you possess the kind of faith that will save you from sin and judgment if you won't provide for the needs of your family. It means that if you fail to provide for your family, you will have done far more than failed to be a husband or a dad or even a man. It means you will have failed to be a Christian. This has to mean that providing for those you love is terribly important to God. And failing to provide financially for the members of your household shows that you have failed to really know Jesus.

A huge mistake I see many young men make is starting too late to provide for their future families. Like any other big opportunity, a lifetime of provision requires preparation. Sadly, most young men underestimate the joy and satisfaction that are found in sacrificing through hard work for the benefit of those you love most.

As it does with every other potentially good thing, the world we live in distorts reality by taking an opportunity to serve others and turning it toward selfishness. We take good things and make them god things. We become worshipers of idols. Jobs and careers and vocations can become very selfish pursuits. I urge you to choose serving others over being selfish. I need you to understand that I'm not asking you to imprison yourself in a life of dutiful drudgery. I am inviting you to take the path of greater joy and satisfaction and freedom: the path of being a provider.

A challenge for you to consider as you start down the path of provision has to do with your perspective. By nature we tend to be nearsighted, or shortsighted, when it comes to work and vocation when we are young. It is so difficult to see beyond a few years as you launch out into your life's work. This is a tragic but common error. It's very difficult today to see where life will lead tomorrow. Make no mistake: tomorrow will bring about a very different reality for your life. God may give you a wife and children who will depend on you to pastor them, protect them, and provide for them. You can start working toward that future today, even before you meet the woman God has for you to spend the rest of your life with. A very few of you will find joy and purpose in remaining single. But even then, providing for more than just yourself will afford you the option to serve others. Living today with no regard to your future is very foolish and potentially painful to you and those you will love most, your dependent family.

I believe the very instant you throw your graduation cap into the air to celebrate commencement from high school, a new chapter in your life truly does begin. In this minute, you morph from a dependent into a prospective provider. Because in that instant you have the potential to be a future husband, father, and, by extension, a future breadwinner, as well. You begin the God-designed process of leaving your father and mother so that you may someday hold fast to your future wife (see Genesis 2:24). You move away from financial dependence on your parents toward financial independence with the view of providing for future dependents someday. If I'm correct in this assumption, it's critically important in the days and weeks following graduation to activate a plan to become a provider.

I have seen far too many young men foolishly deny that anything changes in that moment. So they perpetuate a juvenile life well into their early twenties. Some will even do so into their thirties and forties. Which means, if 1 Timothy 5:8 is inspired and true, they spend these critical years preparing to deny their faith rather than demonstrating that they belong to Jesus by preparing to provide.

Sometimes these young men take low-paying jobs with no future because these jobs are available, convenient, and accessible. Or perhaps they are more pleasant and flexible than other types of work. Dudes form garage bands that take full-time commitments but return only part-time pay, and sometimes they plug away at this kind of life forever. Single young men commit to jobs that are only supposed to support single young men. They become baristas, retail associates, theater managers, etc. While there is nothing wrong with seeing these jobs as temporary to make ends meet while you pursue college or trade school, they are dead ends on the road of lifelong provision. Then, very much like the proverbial frog who slowly boils in the pot while the temperature gradually rises instead of fleeing for his life, you can find yourself on the path to denying your faith in the future. Or perhaps when you come to your senses, you must make a radical yet painful shift later in life, when precious few better options exist.

Brandon began coming to the church I served when he was a high school student. He had many gifts and really enjoyed using them to serve others through church. Volunteering began to take up much of his time. He spent a year as an unpaid intern. He got married and now has two very young sons. But his pursuit of a full-time job with the church hasn't been productive yet. He works multiple jobs to make ends meet and still has years to go to finish his college degree. I had breakfast with him recently and was greatly encouraged to hear that he is forsaking his hunt for a church job so that he can complete his education and land a job that will provide best for his family. Serving and meeting the financial needs of your dependents is a higher priority than serving the church. And while both should be pursued in the right order of ranking, when church service keeps a young man from providing financially for his family, something must change.

So think beyond today as you choose a career path. Think in the long term. Ask Jesus to give you the awesome gift of family; then plan accordingly. Be disciplined and committed to working hard. Sacrifice for the sake of others, even when you don't know your children's names or haven't even met your wife. Someday you will be so glad you did.

Another challenge to young men beginning a career path is selfishness. A selfish man asks too few questions when choosing a career path. He covers the basic questions of *What would I like to do?* and *What am I good at?* These are very important questions. Make no mistake: you will spend many hours in your work over the next forty-plus years, and choosing a vocation that fits you is very important. You should do something you would like to do. You should also do something that fits your skill set so you may do your work very well.

But you must ask yourself a more important question. The answer to this question will be critical in making your career choice. That question is, *How will this work help me provide for my future family?* Research the opportunities your work will give you for advancement and pay increases over time. Research how much money will be needed to provide for a family the size you wish to have, living in the community where you desire to be. Consider that your future wife will serve the family best by devoting herself full-time to the home rather than supplementing your earnings. Then ask yourself after your research, *How will this line of work provide for my future family?* If the answer to that question is "not very well," then you should not spend another moment in consideration of that path. You must choose something today that will be useful tomorrow, or else you are wasting time and falling behind.

I have met many family men who burden their wives and children because of their own career selfishness. They persist in their jobs even when they don't take care of their family's financial needs. They don't have jobs that will allow a wife and mom to stay home and care for children when they arrive. Tragically, these men who don't provide for their families justify their choice to stay in dead-end, faith-denying work with explanations like "I know what I do doesn't pay well, but I like my job." Consider that rationale for a minute. This man is communicating that he would prefer to stay in a job he enjoys at the expense of denying his faith by failing to support his family. That is a huge price to pay for nothing more than an enjoyable, rewarding, and comfortable job.

Stuart has been a lifelong inventor. His career path has been mostly nonconventional. And his family has been mostly dysfunctional. His kids now are grown and have left his unheated and dilapidated home. So has his wife of forty-plus years. In many ways, Stuart has lost that which was most valuable to him on earth—his family—because he refused to consider another trade. He is heartbroken. And while he very well may win his wife back through repentance, he never will be able to provide well for his kids. It is too late.

The true issue here is narcissism. Men who choose jobs that don't provide for their families have an inflated view of their own self-importance and a devalued sense of their wife and children. They also have a depreciated idea of the real and true joy found in sacrifice. In fact, they worship themselves. They seem capable only of seeing life through the lens of self. They sacrifice true joy at the altar of self-worship. Even more tragically, they also place on that very same altar human sacrifices—most commonly their wives and children.

As a young man, you would be best served to consider three paths toward being a provider: military service, college, or trade school. It is a rare opportunity, but could also be effective, for a young man to begin raising capital through immediate and temporary employment that translates into future entrepreneurial capital. But the best providers I have met pick one of these three paths and spend the rest of their lives faithfully walking them out.

If you choose a path in the military, you must do so with a good conscience and a complete understanding of possible outcomes. Go down this road only if you are willing to go to war for your country. It's not an honorable thing to consider only the benefit of this opportunity without factoring in the cost. The military option may lead to leadership development, education, and job training.

I have served alongside many men in the church, both military career men and civilians, who were very well trained in the armed services for a life of provision. Nate is one example. His buddies were having a good time. Some were enjoying their fifth and sixth years of undergraduate studies when Nate enlisted as a marine. He served a tour in Iraq. And he laid a foundation for future family provision. If you are willing to accept the sacrifice that comes with this opportunity, you may experience similar benefits.

There is some debate today about whether or not a college education is beneficial. Personally, I always believe that education is intrinsically helpful. But I am also convinced that not all fields of study are equally productive in terms of financial provision. Many statistics bear that out. You should go to college with a career in mind. According to a recent study, the following majors are the least paying: drama and theater arts; anthropology and archaeology; physical fitness and recreation; fine arts; social work; philosophy and religious studies; psychology; liberal arts; film, video, photography, and music.* You needn't reject these fields of study outright. But you should carefully examine them in light of the potential to obtain a job that will provide for a future family. If there isn't a reasonable way that can be achieved, then abandon those fields as possibilities. Shawn, for example, graduated with an undergraduate degree in history. His ambition was to pursue an advanced degree in church history. In the process of application, he was confronted by career limitations. He went back to college so that he could pursue a career in medicine. Studying something you enjoy simply for the sake of learning is no different than taking a job that is fun but can't provide. In the long run it may be really interesting, but it can also be frivolous and wasteful. It's a spring-set steel trap to avoid.

A college education is a challenge both in terms of time and money. It's a challenge to finish a degree in a reasonable amount of time without racking up an unmanageable amount of student loans. Many young men have to work the equivalent of two jobs, going to class full-time while also working nearly full-time. While I would never endorse this

---

* Anthony P. Carnevale and Ban Cheah, *Hard Times 2013: College Majors, Unemployment and Earnings* (Washington, DC: Georgetown University Center on Education and the Workforce, 2013). You can find the report at www9.georgetown.edu/grad/gppi/hpi/cew/pdfs/HardTimes.2013.2.pdf.

as a plan for a man with a wife, much less children, it can be done for a season of life when you are young—but probably not for more than four or five years. The front-loaded investment of time will reap benefits down the road, when more time and money will be available to serve a family.

I have deep respect and appreciation for men who work skillfully and successfully in the trades. Carpenters, plumbers, electricians, welders, machinists, medical technicians, and other tradesman do very important jobs and may be compensated generously. Much like in any other profession, the key is to begin in the field as soon as possible and to develop a strong skill set that is marketable. One man I know, Craig, started young as a journeyman electrician. He worked very hard while his buddies played. Now, in addition to being a successful electrician, Craig has started his own business, which provides well, not only for his family, but also for all the families of his employees. I think this form of livelihood is what Scripture refers to when it instructs us to "aspire to live quietly, and to mind your own affairs, and to work with your hands, as we instructed you, so that you may walk properly before outsiders and be dependent on no one" (1 Thessalonians 4:11-12).

So What Now?

I encourage you to approach provision with a sense of dignified urgency. You will enter an economy offering a very limited supply of jobs that can enable you to provide for a family. While it may be difficult to accept, landing a job that will someday take care of others is very much like winning a race. False starts, a slow pace, and frequent breaks will keep you from capturing the prize.

Think of this important responsibility like an endurance race. I have completed both marathons and triathlons, and the approach is slightly different. The apex of achievement for an amateur marathon runner is qualifying for the Boston Marathon. Qualification is mostly dependent on achieving an age-specific standardized time in a sanctioned race. In other words, if you meet a certain standard, you will be granted a slot in the big race. But the apex accomplishment for an amateur triathlete is participating in the annual Ironman World Championship in Kona, Hawaii. Competition slots in this race are also captured at qualifying events, but the format is different from qualifying for the Boston Marathon. A good time doesn't guarantee a place in the race. You must earn a place in the event by actually beating others. In a marathon qualification, you are largely competing against yourself or against a standard of qualification. In a triathlon, you are racing against others—and unless you beat them, you won't make it to the big race.

Securing a job that will provide for your family is more like the Ironman Triathlon than the Boston Marathon. There are only so many slots available, and you must beat out others to win one of them. So please understand that for every minute you waste and every opportunity you blow, you are falling behind others who will beat you and take your spot. This doesn't mean you have to beat others up to win the race. But you must do your very best to prepare and present yourself as the most qualified. And do it by faith, trusting the Holy Spirit to give you the strength, wisdom, and endurance you don't naturally possess.

Last, I can't overemphasize how important it is to have a clear motive in working toward being able to provide for a family someday. While competition and pride may push you toward your goal, they won't satisfy you or please Jesus. But love will. Through the Holy Spirit, Jesus can give you a supernatural love that allows you to serve the most important people in your life—people you may not even know yet. Trust him and work hard for those who may someday depend on you. Your salvation doesn't depend on it; that's solely reliant on the person and work of Jesus. But your salvation is *verified* by your being a man who provides financially for the members of his home. This is terribly serious—serious enough that you must get started on a good plan. Work hard and work smart today for those who will depend on you tomorrow. Your faith will be proven true, your joy will be complete, and your family someday will be thankful.

Here are five practical next steps.

First, pray. Ask the Holy Spirit to direct you to the path he desires for you as you prepare to provide for others. Trust him to provide that direction.

Second, pursue the counsel of those who have spiritual authority over you. If you have a dad, ask him for direction. Seek input from your pastor or other leaders in your church.

Third, pick a path. Start walking. Trust the providence of the God you worship to redirect you if needed. But walk through the open doors and be diligent. Don't second-guess yourself. Be resilient and persistent. Walking down the same path for a long time typically produces the best results.

Fourth, plan for the future. Open up the calendar and calculator apps on your phone and go to work. Have goals in mind. Think beyond yourself. Plan for your future family.

Fifth, partner with someone who has seen it, done it, and been there—someone who can consult with you and hold you accountable to stick with your plan. If you don't have a trustworthy dad to walk you through this plan, seek out another older man whom you respect to help you. Many of the skills in providing for others are caught rather than taught. So put yourself in the best place to learn from someone you'd like to follow. Be bold in this. You may not see it yet, but you will be just as helpful to him as he is to you. I have been on the other side of this partnership for years now and can tell you few things are more rewarding than helping young men prepare to serve their future families well.

6

CITIZEN

Dear Son,

I was talking to a young woman the other day about becoming a Christian. She had a growing awareness of her sin. She had been attending church for a while. She was fascinated by the Bible. She was even more intrigued by Jesus and the audacious claims he made. She had been living with a man without being married, and out of her conviction, she broke off the relationship and moved in with some of her girlfriends.

Although I was encouraged by her growing awareness of sin and interest in Jesus, she wasn't yet a believer. Morally aligning your life with the teachings of Jesus apart from being forgiven and freed from sin by him does a person very little good.

As we talked, I was certain she understood what it meant to become a Christian. I also was convinced she wanted to become a Christian. Yet something was holding her back that wasn't obvious to me. Finally, I just asked her in a straightforward tone, "Why don't you become a Christian today? What is holding you back?"

Her answer caught me off guard. As a matter of fact, it was funny, and I couldn't contain my laughter. She looked me in the eye with all sincerity and said, "Pastor Dave, I'm not ready to become a Christian yet because I am still not ready to become a Republican. Pray for me!" Once I stopped laughing and she stopped being annoyed by my laughter, I explained that being a Republican isn't a prerequisite to becoming a Christian. She was relieved, and together we prayed that Jesus would forgive her sin and that, as her Lord, would guide her in a new life.

As we finished our discussion, she asked me once more for the sake of clarity, "So I don't have to become a Republican now?" I wanted to give her a serious response. I told her this: "No. You don't have to become a Republican. But with Jesus' help, you must become a good citizen."

Son, if you were with us now, you would be old enough to vote. I would have liked talking about the issues and taking you to the polling place for the first time or dropping off your ballot in the mail. Whether you had grown up to be a Republican, a Democrat, or an Independent or had started your own party, I would have taught you what I know about being a good citizen of the United States, and of the state of Washington, and of the city of Seattle. Maybe one day you'll be teaching me about citizenship in heaven.

I love you and will join you there someday,

Dad

. . .

We live in a very broken world. Poverty, oppression, disease, starvation, and war are all too common. It's a harsh world with little respect for human life. It is a world that is mostly opposed to Jesus and resists his rule. Yet according to the Bible, we, as Christian men, are to live in this sinful world as good citizens. I've been striving toward that calling for decades, and trust me, it's not easy.

Pastor Titus, much like Pastor Timothy, worked closely with the apostle Paul. He had a tough assignment in leading the church on Crete. The apostle had this to say about the people of Crete: "One of the Cretans, a prophet of their own, said, 'Cretans are always liars, evil beasts, lazy gluttons.' This testimony is true" (Titus 1:12-13). Not the easiest place to live or do pastoral ministry. Maybe even a tougher culture to live in as a young Christian man. It wouldn't be easy to live as a growing Christian among liars, evil beasts, and lazy gluttons. It would be even harder to live in a way that benefited the Cretans in your midst.

It's against this cultural backdrop that Paul writes with instructions for Titus regarding the Christians in Crete:

"Remind them to be submissive to rulers and authorities, to be obedient, to be ready for every good work, to speak evil of no one, to avoid quarreling, to be gentle, and to show perfect courtesy toward all people" (Titus 3:1-2). That's not exactly the plan I would have proposed if I were Paul. But it most certainly was the one he received from God and passed on to Pastor Titus and the church in Crete.

If you're a young man today, you're entering manhood in the same cultural stream I did twenty-some years ago. But much has changed. While the stream may be the same one I first entered, the water you step into is radically different. I came of age during the Ronald Reagan era of American politics. Political conservatism was in vogue. Evangelicalism seemed to be making huge strides forward. It was the heyday of the Christian Right. Christian ethics were widely accepted if not honored. Believe it or not, many of those who didn't know Jesus believed that his teachings should be observed.

Your entry point in America is very different. Human secularism has become our national religion. Many consider evangelicals to be as sophisticated as those who believed that the earth is flat or that bleeding with leeches was the way to heal all physical ailments. Cultural and political opposition to the views of Christians are becoming stronger and more organized with each passing day. For example, tolerance is the highest or one of the highest values in our society today. But Bible-believing Christians largely are excluded from the tolerance fest. Try this on for size: just publicly post your opposition to abortion or gay marriage as a Christian on social media channels and wait for the accusations that you're waging a "war on women" or being "homophobic." In other words, all beliefs and opinions can be tolerated except from people who are narrow minded enough to believe the Bible.

You can see the "p word"—*persecution*—coming on the horizon like a dark and distant threatening storm slowly blowing in your direction. It will arrive someday soon and change some of the freedoms we have enjoyed in the past.

Yet even with all the current cultural and political trends, our present environment is far more hospitable and welcoming toward our Christian convictions than the one early Christians in Crete encountered. It wasn't long after Paul wrote those words to Titus that Christian-focused persecution exploded under Emperor Nero, which makes Paul's words on how to live as good citizens in an evil world even more poignant and applicable today.

> *Remind them to be submissive to rulers and authorities, to be obedient, to be ready for every good work, to speak evil of no one, to avoid quarreling, to be gentle, and to show perfect courtesy toward all people.*
>
> —Titus 3:1-2

We Christians are to be submissive to authority, to be ready for good works, and to speak to and about others with grace. These are essentials if we are to be good citizens of heaven *and* earth.

The first thing we must be is submissive and obedient

to governing authority, which is not at all a popular senti-
ment among Americans, particularly those of the millennial
generation. But even the most radicalized man can bring
himself to submit to authority when he's living under the
authority of a good and democratically elected government.
How would you like to submit to a ruler who was out to kill
you for your faith?

Crete, like most of the ancient Near East in the early
years of Christianity, was governed by the evil empire of
Rome. According to Christian tradition, the very man who
penned these words, the apostle Paul, was beheaded by the
insane Emperor Nero within years of writing this letter. So
in a shocking twist of fate, Paul is calling on Christians to
submit and obey the very government that eventually will
execute him for preaching Jesus. And he seems to know this
in advance (see 2 Timothy 4:6-8).

It's very important that we men who follow Jesus obey
his teachings, first in our hearts and then with our thoughts,
words, and actions in regard to the governmental authority
(civic, county, state, and federal) God has placed over us.
The word in these verses that is translated "submission" is a
military term that describes living within the framework of
a chain of command. The Bible makes it very clear that God
is legitimately at the apex of every human government on
earth (see Romans 13:1-7, for example). Obedience to God
requires obedience to those in his chain of command. This
includes keeping every law, no matter how obscure and seem-
ingly insignificant, and paying every tax that is due. The only

freedom we have to disobey the government is when we are personally required by authorities to disobey God's revealed will. (In a case like that, *they* are the ones who have broken the chain of command.)

There are many people in Scripture who are good examples of disobeying the government for God's glory. Exodus 1 records the civil disobedience of the Jewish midwives, who were instructed to murder all boys born to Jewish women. The midwives feared God, so they disobeyed Pharaoh. Their action pleased God, and he rewarded them. Joshua 2 tells of Rahab, who refused to give up the Jewish spies to the authorities. The spies most certainly would have been killed by the king of Jericho if not for her actions. Hebrews 11:31 affirms Rahab's disobedience as an act of faith. The book of Daniel has perhaps the most famous story: Daniel refused to cease worshiping God, so he was thrown in the lion's den. God sent his angel to save Daniel, and pagan King Darius ended up praising God (see chapter 6).

But civil disobedience is the exception, not the rule. Except in extreme circumstances, we are to honor those who serve the public good through governing. Honor is shaping our attitudes, words, and actions toward elected officials. This should impact the bumper stickers we choose to put on our cars as well as what we post to Facebook. It certainly doesn't mean we can't engage in civil debate in a democratic society, but all debate must be honoring to and respectful of those in authority—especially those who disagree with us most strongly! The shrill and vitriolic protest coming from people who profess faith in Jesus does nothing to honor God. Imagine the change that could take place if Christian young men would lead the charge in resetting the tone of political disagreement in this country. You might face opposition from those with the reddest faces and loudest voices, but you would have the truth of the Bible in your corner. And that is no small thing.

Imagine the change that could take place if Christian young men would lead the charge in resetting the tone of political disagreement in this country.

Not only are Christians to be submissive to government, we also are to be "ready for every good work" (Titus 3:1). This means that as Christian men, we live as conscientious and active citizens dedicated to the common good of our communities. For you personally, that includes being a good steward of your time, talent, and money so you always have a margin to give to those in need. In a democracy such as we live in, it means you vote and participate in a way that takes into consideration the greatest good for the most people. Don't fall into the selfishness of special-interest politics that have too often ignored the needs of others in our country. "Be ready for every good work" in the workplace, classroom, neighborhood, city, and voting booth.

The easiest place to begin doing good work is where you live, work, and play: your dorm, apartment complex, classroom, office, or neighborhood. Square one of being a solid Christian man is taking responsibility for the well-being of others. Look for fellow renters, work associates, classmates, or nearby homeowners who need a hand caring for their property, doing their work, or making ends meet. Save up some money to help those in need. Tell those you help that every good work you do is because of Jesus. We can illustrate God's grace in Jesus toward us through good works. But we can communicate the gospel in a manner that saves lost people only through good words. Do both to make sure those you are caring for are clear about Jesus.

One thing we can't be is angry and antagonistic with our words. Specifically, according to this text, we are "to speak evil of no one." We are not to engage in character assassination, slander, or gossip. Feeling convicted yet? I'm sorry to be the one to break it to you, but your age group is mostly known for passion, idealism—and the regular loss of discretion.

Trash talk has become a culturally acceptable art form. It's in music, movies, and sports. Even in the Christian community, young men can often become well known through creatively yet cuttingly putting down their peers. But words have enormous power. They may be used to build up or tear down. Using words to hurt others is just as damaging as using your fists to do the same.

I still cringe when I consider some of the things I said to and about others as a young man. My social and political commentary was immature and ill informed. I so wish I could take those things back. Fortunately, not many people listened to me then! Those who did were smart not to take me too seriously. I seldom venture onto Facebook without seeing your peers repeating the folly of my youth. However, today's consequences are far more serious. Unhelpful words that make their way into cyberspace become permanent, like bad tattoos. To undo them takes money and involves pain, and those closest to you will struggle to forget your stupidity.

Worse yet, our angry and careless words may turn into an obstacle over which unbelievers trip as they make their way toward the pull of Jesus' grace. I have spent much time over the years telling others about Jesus. Most of them had really strange misconceptions about him. Almost all the non-Christians I've shared with have formed stereotypes of Christians that cause them to be cold toward the faith. Those errors and stereotypes were forged from angry or hurtful words coming out of the mouths of Christians.

So avoid arguing with those who don't yet know Jesus. While you must be prepared to defend what you believe when you are asked to explain, you need not be provocative toward those who don't believe as you do. While I am open to the possibility of their existence, I have yet to meet a single Christian who was led to faith in Jesus through the angry words of an argumentative family member, friend, or coworker. Not one.

Understand that when you argue with Christians and unbelievers on social media, you are fighting in front of others who will be turned off by your faith rather than tuned in to hearing more of what you have to say. In this realm, tone and posture are so important. Speak plainly, with an

inviting voice and arms open to receive anyone who will listen. Don't be fearful or tentative. Be bold. But be smart.

Our disposition toward those who disagree with us is so
important to God. Too many Christians in our culture are
arrogant and proud toward those who don't yet know Jesus.
They are condemning and judg-
mental and betray the very grace
they profess to believe.

*Almost all the non-
Christians I've shared
with have formed
stereotypes of Christians
that cause them to be
cold toward the faith.
Those errors and
stereotypes were forged
from angry or hurtful
words coming out of the
mouths of Christians.*

Being humble doesn't mean
you don't have strong convictions.
Quite the opposite: humility is
based on confidently knowing
who you are and knowing who
others are in light of who God
says you are. There is a vast difference between someone who is
uncertain and someone who is
humble. Humility enables you
to engage someone who disagrees
with you calmly and respectfully because you know the out-
come doesn't rely on your strength and ability. It also cush-
ions the blow of rejection. If an opponent disagrees with your
faith, he or she is rejecting Jesus, too. There is solace to be
found in the company of rejects.

Last, we are to be gentle and courteous. Certainly those
descriptions should characterize the conversations we've just
been talking about. But I think gentleness may be particularly
meaningful to those who are most vulnerable to oppression

and injustice. There are many who fit that category, but right now let's focus on women and children. James, the half-brother of Jesus, said it this way: "Religion that is pure and undefiled before God, the Father, is this: to visit orphans and widows in their affliction, and to keep oneself unstained from the world" (James 1:27). You can be a good citizen by looking out for the needs of women and children who are without men in their families, namely husbands and fathers, to protect them. And while there are certainly opportunities to serve widows and orphans across your community and around the world, I invite you to concern yourself with the plight of single moms in the church. Show them respect. Help them in practical ways. Do chores, run errands, fix broken cars, and do some heavy lifting for them. Refuse to exploit or allow anyone else to take advantage of their vulnerabilities. Help model what it means to be a man who loves Jesus in front of boys and girls who don't have a man leading their family. Jesus loves justice and hates oppression and abuse. Learn to love what he loves and hate what he hates. Most important, love the people he loves who need your help.

So What Now?

You are to live as a good citizen in a bad world. God has called you to this juxtaposed existence. But this strange calling isn't without reason. Paul follows up his instruction to Christians living among beastly Cretans with this compelling thought:

We ourselves were once foolish, disobedient, led
astray, slaves to various passions and pleasures,
passing our days in malice and envy, hated by others
and hating one another. But when the goodness
and loving kindness of God our Savior appeared,
he saved us, not because of works done by us in
righteousness, but according to his own mercy, by
the washing of regeneration and renewal of the Holy
Spirit, whom he poured out on us richly through
Jesus Christ our Savior, so that being justified by his
grace we might become heirs according to the hope
of eternal life.

TITUS 3:3-7

Two critically important things tether us to the truth of
God as we consider the ungodly status of unbelievers.

First, we were just like them and would still be like them
had God not intervened. There was a point in time when you
and I and all men opposed everything to do with God. We
rebelled against him, and if we were saved after an age where
we were old enough to have made enemies, we, too, would
have known people who claimed their God could save us from
the sin we denied carrying. We were helpless to change our fate
and would have continued down a path of hateful destruction
just like the path those who resist us travel down each day.

Try to accurately see unbelievers for who they are. They
aren't enemies. They are helpless captives of war, blindly carrying out the battle plans of our enemy. We don't kill prisoners

of war; we work to free them. We must resist the strong temptation of fighting the culture war. We must enlist other young men to join us as we free captives from the spiritual holocaust.

Second, we didn't save ourselves. If we had, then we might have a little space to brag and to look down on others who have yet to be liberated. But our salvation was solely the work of God our Savior through Jesus Christ and the Holy Spirit. All we added to the mix was sin. This should be incredibly humbling. As we look upon a world of people still lost in captivity, there is no room for pride. There is no place for self-righteousness—most certainly not toward those who are like us in every way possible except that they have yet to be rescued.

You are a dual citizen. You belong to King Jesus and his coming Kingdom. You also are a temporary passport holder here on this earth. You must live as a good citizen in a sinful world. You must live a Jesus-centered life among those who hate him, his truth, and most passionately, his people. You must live among "liars, evil beasts and lazy gluttons." How will you live among the Cretans? It means a lot to Jesus.

7

MEMBER

Dear Son,

I've just come home after another Easter at Mars Hill Church. It was a huge celebration of Jesus' resurrection. We had more than twenty thousand people attending services across all the locations. I was particularly busy with my role as an online host for our global extended family watching these services through the Internet. And while there were many great things to be excited about today, one image stands out among all the others: I love watching people who have just met Jesus get baptized!

I am encouraged by the people being baptized. To view their expressions as they rise from the water is incredible. I also never get tired of the faces of loved ones seeing someone they care about be baptized. Family members, friends, coworkers, and neighbors have tear-streaked faces as they watch someone they have prayed for and pursued meet Jesus and publicly profess a brand-new faith. But here's the image that captures my heart the most: I love watching those performing the baptism as they are overcome by the realization that another brother or sister is being welcomed into the family of faith. Despite the fact that I've watched this scene unfold thousands of times, it still wrecks me. It makes all the hard work, heartache, frustration, and disappointment that go along with pastoral ministry worthwhile. It actually makes them seem pretty miniscule when compared with the magnitude of an expanding family!

Son, if you still were here today, I would find deep pride in knowing you were an active member in a local church. I have watched each of your college-age sisters leave home and get involved in local churches. I am sure you would have done the same.

While my view into Jesus' work in the church here and now is amazing, your seat is even better. May his Kingdom come here on earth, where I am, as it is where you are, in heaven! Until that happens, I am tired and need to get some sleep.

I love you, Son,
Dad

. . .

A young man recently sought my counsel about which church he and his wife should attend. He was disappointed in some of the things that were going on in the church he had been attending. He was hearing counsel from leaders that didn't square with the Bible. He also was largely being ignored in his development as a leader. So he came to me asking for my input. He was asking legitimate questions. To move the conversation along, it seemed important to take a big step back in an attempt to see the larger picture. I asked him the question, "What should a young man look for in a church?"

I was assuming a lot with that question. I may be taking for granted that a young man sees value in being a member of a church in the first place. It seems to me that young men mostly are absent in church. This is tragic and explains why the American church is rapidly losing influence.

I can think of nothing more important to your spiritual well-being than being actively involved in the life of a local church. Adam, a guy I met several years ago, found this out. He had bounced around different churches for several years. He was disillusioned because of some bad experiences. But he quickly committed himself to the local church. He began to flourish. He grew in obedience to Jesus, and he helped others to do the same. But before too long, he decided to move on once again. I saw him a few years later, and he relayed to me how his spiritual growth had been stunted since he left. We prayed together, and he committed to returning to the church. And once again, he began to grow and serve.

To consider yourself a Christian while being detached from a local church is such an obvious anomaly, the Bible hardly approaches the subject. The writers of the New Testament do address the issue of people being a part of the local church yet missing gatherings. For instance, Hebrews 10:24-25 warns against being away from one's church: "Let us consider how to stir up one another to love and good works, not neglecting to meet together, as is the habit of some, but encouraging one another, and all the more as you see the Day drawing near." But the idea that someone would choose to avoid church altogether and still consider himself a Christian seems to be such a ridiculous concept that it's never directly confronted.

Yet that is exactly what many young Christian men are doing today: living ridiculously. To make matters worse, with the assistance of unlimited Internet content and opinions, you always can find someone to agree with positions that are foolish and contrary to the Bible. There are those out there who dismiss the biblical importance of the local church. They believe in churchless Christians much like other Internet bloggers believe in and post pictures of unicorns and aliens.

Avoiding actively participating in a local church is akin to avoiding eating nutritious food, drinking water, sleeping, and breathing clean air. You do so to your own eventual and certain demise. It not only hurts the young men who are missing in church but also stunts the health of the local church. Being a good member of a Bible-believing local church is a nonnegotiable essential for your spiritual health and growth.

So if being a member of a local church is undeniably important, what factors should you consider when choosing a church? A not-so-obvious passage of Scripture may prove to be really helpful in answering this question. Take a look at the words Paul writes to young Pastor Timothy: "Keep a close watch on yourself and on the teaching. Persist in this, for by so doing you will save both yourself and your hearers" (1 Timothy 4:16). It would seem, based on this text, that the spiritual health of the members of a church (the hearers) is a direct result of the spiritual vitality of their preaching pastor. Or more

Being a good member of a Bible-believing local church is a non-negotiable essential for your spiritual health and growth.

specifically, preaching pastors who practice self-examination, closely looking after their own doctrinal convictions and lifestyles for alignment with Jesus and his gospel, produce church members who do the same. Nothing is more important in the selection of a church home than the integrity of the teaching ministry and personal life of the preaching pastor. So choose your home church with care.

According to Paul, there are only two types of teaching: healthy and unhealthy. As a matter of fact, the word that is translated "sound" when the Bible talks about "sound teaching" (see 2 Timothy 4:3, for example) is the very same word from which we get our English word *hygiene*. Over and over again, Paul points out that healthy teaching is focused primarily on the person and work of Jesus. This is so important to understand.

The Bible isn't a book of a thousand principles to live by;

it is a book about the one person to live for: Jesus. He, himself, says this about the Bible. When questioned by angry and cynical religious leaders, Jesus gave us this way of interpreting the Old Testament: "You search the Scriptures because you think that in them you have eternal life; and it is they that bear witness about me" (John 5:39). Then after his resurrection from the dead, he walked down a long road with two disciples who didn't recognize him at first. According to the Bible, "beginning with Moses and all the Prophets, he interpreted to them in all the Scriptures the things concerning himself" (Luke 24:27). What an incredible truth this text reveals: the entire Old Testament from Genesis (Moses) through Malachi (Prophets) contains truths about Jesus.

The entire New Testament also is about Jesus. The Gospels reveal his earthly life, death, and resurrection. The book of Acts is about the continuation of Jesus' mission by his church. Romans through Jude are about the amazing implications of Jesus' finished work and coming Kingdom in the lives of believers, the church, and the world. According to the prophetic book of Revelation, the very last book of the Bible, "the testimony of Jesus is the spirit of prophecy" (Revelation 19:10). The history of the world as we know it unfolds in Jesus.

Start to finish, the Bible is a book about Jesus. So it only stands to reason that a preaching pastor who is closely watching his Bible teaching will talk a lot about Jesus. But my own disappointing experience is that you can listen to a lot of sermons in which Jesus may make a cameo appearance but is seldom the hero. Many sermons in evangelical churches today are about four things: prosperity, morality, politics, and prophetic speculation. Accordingly, many sermons miss Paul's mark of healthy or hygienic teaching that nurtures pastors and members while saving souls.

Prosperity preaching is the first potential problem you may run into in evangelical churches. It's not that the Bible never addresses prosperity. Jesus himself said this: "I came that they may have life and have it abundantly" (John 10:10). Jesus healed the sick, freed the demonically oppressed, and raised the dead. And he certainly spoke a lot about money.

But personal prosperity isn't the central theme of the Bible, because people aren't the main point—Jesus is. As a matter of fact, Jesus and the authors of the New Testament say considerably more about suffering, sickness, and persecution than they do of health and wealth.

How do you know if a church has an unhealthy focus on prosperity? Here are a couple of key things to listen for. First, is Jesus the focal point of the sermon, or are you? The Bible is a book about Jesus, so an accurate biblical message should end on Jesus as the big idea, not on you or me. Second, are suffering and hardship addressed as *paths toward* or *obstacles to* growth? Does suffering demonstrate the presence or absence of faith? Suffering most frequently is the means by which a follower learns to trust more deeply in Jesus—which takes us back to question one.

I have met many young men who attend prosperity-preaching churches. They seem to genuinely love Jesus. They worship passionately. They believe Jesus will do great things for them and through them. They aren't bad men at all. They aren't to be rejected or resisted. They are true brothers to be received warmly with love. But they are stunted in growth much like you would be if all you ever consumed in your formative years were sugar-laden snacks and fast food. Are they happy? Most definitely, yes. Are they healthy and well developed? Probably not so much.

Moralistic preaching is a second problem you may encounter, and it's both subtle and dangerous. It is subtle because the Bible does indeed instruct us on how to live. Make no mistake, there are things you should do and not do in order to please God. But moralistic preaching places the emphasis on the things you should and shouldn't do *so that Jesus will love you*. Moralism says that Jesus will love you when you stop looking at porn. But the Bible teaches that Jesus does love you if you belong to him. So *because* he loves you, you are empowered to stop looking at porn. You don't abandon porn to make him love you; you do so because he already does! Moralism misses the point that we live as Christians to be like Jesus, obeying God our Father in the power of the Holy Spirit because he already loves us, not so someday he will love us if we follow all the rules. I hope you see the contrast. It may seem to be an issue of semantics, but the distinction between unhealthy moralism and the healthy teaching of the gospel is worlds apart.

How can you know if a pastor preaches moralism?

For one thing, moralism makes role models out of characters in the Bible. This kind of preaching challenges you to be more like Moses and David (except for that adulterous and murderous episode, of course!) and not to be like Pharaoh or Goliath. To be sure, there are patterns to follow and to avoid in the Bible, but healthy preaching has Jesus as the ultimate hero of every Bible story. All the other characters just point to him. And the big idea is to be more like Jesus, as the Holy Spirit applies his obedience to you by faith. Unhealthy moralism is about you and me paying back a debt of obedience to Jesus, who graciously died for our sin. But healthy preaching highlights that you and I are falling deeper into the debt of Jesus daily. Moralism is about doing more and trying harder. Healthy preaching is about declaring to sinners that their enormous debt has been canceled by Jesus' perfect and finished work on the cross. Moralism is about penance—doing makeup work to demonstrate how sorry you are for messing up. Healthy preaching is about repentance—turning in sorrow back to Jesus' work.

The biggest problem with moralism is that it doesn't work. Moralism may change behavior temporarily, but it cannot change the heart eternally. External change is futile, because people are wired from the inside out. External modification apart from inward transformation will not sustain. Moralism leads to defeat, shame, and guilt. Temporary obedience may be mixed into this cycle. But it's the type of obedience that isn't impressive to God. Who needs church for that? We can find enough examples of false obedience outside the church on our own.

A third pitfall you may find is that some churches are nothing more than platforms for the talking points of conservative politics. Fewer churches attempt to do the same from a Left-leaning political position. But both approaches tend to miss Jesus' take on human nature. Scripture gives us this insight into how Jesus views people: "When he was in Jerusalem at the Passover Feast, many believed in his name when they saw the signs that he was doing. But Jesus on his part did not entrust himself to them, because he knew all people and needed no one to bear witness about man, for he himself knew what was in man" (John 2:23-25). Central to healthy teaching is the biblical concept of human inability. The Bible teaches that the human species cannot in any way remedy a broken relationship with God or live pleasingly in his sight without his intervention. Salvation cannot be legislated.

It's usually pretty easy to tell if a church is more focused on politics than on Jesus. All you have to do is listen to the story from the pulpit. A political church will write Jesus into the current political narrative. In other words, the preacher may say things like, "How would Jesus vote on this issue?" A biblical church, in contrast, writes the current political narrative into Jesus' story. It acknowledges that regardless of what dire consequences people may predict if such-and-such a bill passes (or fails) or so-and-so gets elected (or doesn't), Jesus is the ultimate King. His Kingdom is advancing regardless of the political climate.

I believe preachers who stand before the churches they lead and preach politics from the Left or Right want the same noble thing. They desire a better world for the people they love. But they also make the same really big mistake: political movements don't save people. They may, at best, apart from Jesus, simply make life a little more tolerable as we all make our way toward the eternal torments of hell. This reality totally obscures the noble desire like a solar eclipse. Only healthy teaching proclaimed regularly and patiently— teaching that through Jesus, God saves sinners who cannot save themselves—changes the hearts of people. Only people with changed hearts truly can make this world a better and changed place.

A fourth problem to watch out for is prophetic specula-tion. Its unhelpful focus can eclipse healthy teaching. Similar to the other forms of misguided preaching, this genre isn't without biblical support. A significant amount of the Bible is about informing God's people of what to expect in the future. But the big idea with true biblical prophecy is that all things are going to conclude with Jesus ruling forever over his people, composed of all ethnicities who've trusted in him throughout human history, in a re-created and sinless world. When he returns to completely inaugurate his Kingdom, everyone who is living will be surprised.

Popular prophecy becomes obsessed with the puzzle pieces to this final picture as revealed in the Bible. So current events are hashed out in light of geopolitical shifts and verses are found from books like Daniel, Matthew, and Revelation in an attempt to mix and match until the day and hour of Jesus' return is nailed down. Almost every sermon revolves around the political state of Israel. The teachings are illustrated with charts that have lots of brackets, parentheses, and illustrations that look like they have been lifted out of comic books. And then the preacher makes predictions about the day of Jesus' return. Which is exactly contrary to what Jesus said about his second coming: "Concerning that day and hour no one knows, not even the angels of heaven, nor the Son, but the Father only" (Matthew 24:36). Because no one knows when Jesus is coming, we are to be ready for his return by being as mature as possible through the hearing and believing in healthy teaching. You can see the unhelpful place this type of preaching is going. By being obsessed with lesser details, we miss the "big *E*" on the eye chart.

A preacher who keeps a close watch on his teaching will be an enormous help to you. He will speak often of Jesus. Jesus' perfect life, sacrificial death, victorious resurrection, and glorious ascension will be more than your weekly clue that the message is almost over and you can start thinking about lunch. Instead, Jesus will be at the heart of every sermon each and every week. You will be asked for something other than trying harder and doing more for Jesus. You will be compelled to turn from your sin and trust once more in King Jesus for forgiveness and the freedom to worship him with all of your life. You will be challenged to repent.

While the gospel is taught in the pulpit, the pastor needs to live in light of the message he's delivering. When someone is transformed by the message of Jesus dying on the cross for our sins, he lives differently. He not only talks the talk, he walks the walk. A pastor's private attitudes, thoughts, words, and actions are just as important as his public words. It's in keeping a close watch over both that he benefits those he shepherds the most.

I believe you can best evaluate the spiritual life of a pastor by observing the way in which he leads himself, his wife, and his children toward Jesus. The most effective pastors are those men who most consistently point people toward Jesus with their words and actions. They do it best and most in the relationships that are closest to them.

A pastor who leads himself to Jesus will be a man who regularly and openly repents of sin. A pastor who is walking closely to Jesus will be burdened by his own sin. He

Keep a close watch on yourself and on the teaching. Persist in this, for by so doing you will save both yourself and your hearers.
—1 Timothy 4:16

will shed tears over sin. He will be quick to own his failures before his people. This means he practices what he preaches.

Beware of one-dimensional pastors. The pastor who seems to have a vibrant relationship with Jesus but is lacking in doctrinal precision isn't a man you should follow. He will stunt your spiritual development through his sloppy preaching. While there certainly will be value in what you can gain from his example, you need much more than that to reach maturity as a Christian. You need to live on a steady diet of God's Word rightly explained and applied.

The pastor who is a great public preacher of the gospel but

privately doesn't turn from sin to trust in Jesus isn't helpful to you either. I'm personally aware of more than a few preachers who hit home runs routinely in the pulpit only to strike out in addressing obvious sin in their lives. One man I have listened to extensively never has repented of any sin publicly, that I am aware of. It's no surprise to me that when members of his church relocate to cities I've lived in, the leaders representing the churches they visit cringe. These former members have a reputation of being great doctrinally but proudly self-righteous and hypercritical of other churches. They have become just like their leader, strong doctrinally but weak in life.

A preacher who leads himself effectively toward Jesus will acknowledge and correct his preaching errors. He will seek forgiveness from those he serves when he leads in a manner unworthy of Jesus in word or deed. He will openly confess weaknesses, fears, and insecurities among other leaders and to members when appropriate, so that you will know how to pray for him in his role as a Christian, husband, father, and pastor. He will be open about his weaknesses and vulnerable about the struggles in his heart, home, and church.

There's another aspect to finding a great preacher, and that's how he treats his family. A preacher worth following also is a man who has a marriage worth emulating. Healthy church leadership begins at home. His wife will flourish under his spiritual authority. She, too, will love Jesus. She will love hearing the Bible proclaimed by her husband week in and week out. She will profoundly love the church as a fellow member.

The most recognizable trait you will want to see in a pastor as he relates to his wife is unchallenged devotion. He will be committed to her alone above all other women, spiritually, emotionally, and physically. He will love her more than he loves his position in ministry and the church he's called to lead. It will be most obvious that nothing among other human relationships is close to the one he enjoys with her.

A preacher worth following also will lead his children well. They definitely won't be perfect, but they will be sensitive to Jesus and submissive to Dad. According to the Bible's reasoning, "he must manage his own household well, with all dignity keeping his children submissive, for if someone does not know how to manage his own household, how will he care for God's church?" (1 Timothy 3:4-5). He will delight in his kids. Spending time with them won't be a duty for him to fulfill. If his kids are burdensome to him, you and the rest of the church will be as well. But if he loves his own children and leads them well, chances are great he will do the same for his spiritual kids.

Some churches that you consider may be too large for you to personally know the preaching pastor. That's okay as long as you can interview others in leadership within that church who personally can vouch for the spiritual health of the preacher, the strength of his marriage, and the well-being of his home. If the church is smaller and the pastor is available, take the necessary time to interview him and be certain he is practicing a close watch over his teaching ministry and his life.

Choosing a church is an incredibly important decision. The only choices you will make that will have greater impact are your profession of faith and whom you decide to marry. Please choose carefully and wisely. You never will find a perfect church. It doesn't exist. But you certainly will find a pastor worth following. If he carefully watches over his teaching and life, he will validate his own salvation and help you do the same. Nothing is more joyful than living in the assurance of a strong relationship with God through Jesus.

So What Now?

Here are a few practical next steps to get you started if you don't have a church home and don't know anyone you trust who can recommend one for you.

First, look at the websites of churches in your area. Pay careful attention to an emphasis on Jesus. If Jesus is sufficiently central, then look for a doctrinal statement. Read it over with a Bible in hand. Then listen to a few of the pastor's sermons if they are available. Are they based on the Bible? Do they emphasize the person and work of Jesus? Does the pastor speak regularly about sin and repentance? If so, then it is time to pay this church a visit.

Second, as you visit, confirm that the good things you have seen online are evident on Sunday. Mostly, evaluate whether or not the pastor is a man you would wish to emulate. Be patient, as this may take some time to figure out. But don't be negligent, either.

Third, ask the appropriate sources about two issues: What are the qualifications of the church leaders and what are the requirements for becoming a member? Hopefully, you will be directed to the important passages of 1 Timothy 3 and Titus 1 regarding qualified church leaders. And the requirements and expectations of membership also will be clear. Keep in mind that a church that expects much of her members usually is a church that helps much toward growing in obedience to Jesus.

8

—

HUSBAND

Dear Son,

I was confident and expectant during the five months
of my engagement to your mom. At least I was
until our wedding day. During the hours leading
up to the ceremony, I was gripped with anxiety and
fear. I wasn't worried about spending the rest of
my life with your mom. I loved her very much and
was entirely confident she was a gift to me from
Jesus. I couldn't wait to marry her. But I was afraid
I somehow would mess up the ceremony. I might
forget my lines. I might trip walking up the steps to
the altar. I might faint by standing straight-legged for
too long. I might even vomit on your mom's beautiful
white dress.

But I swallowed my fear and my nausea. I made it
through the ceremony without a stutter or a stumble.

I never lost consciousness. It was an incredibly meaningful experience. I spent most of it worshiping Jesus for being so kind as to save me and give me a woman who loved him first and me next. I was more aware of what I was saying and what others were saying and singing than I had been at any other time in my life. I was dialed in. The service ended quickly, we took a few more pictures, and then we greeted our guests at the reception. We were married on a snowy December night in Lubbock, Texas. Only our closest friends and family members attended, which made the experience all the more special.

Your mom and I made our way to her metallic-blue Mustang getaway car through a gauntlet of rice throwers. We drove a few minutes down across town and checked into the honeymoon suite at a nearby hotel. We would catch a flight and head for a Caribbean cruise early the next morning.

I risk telling you what happened next knowing it would make you really uncomfortable. I feel awkward writing it down, so I can only guess how awkward it would be to read about this stuff involving your mom and dad. But here it goes. . . .

After your mom and I sat in the room for a while, recounting our favorite scenes from the wedding and reception, we went into separate changing rooms to get ready to go to bed together for the first time in our relationship. Once again, I was a nervous wreck.

Vomit would probably ruin what was going to happen next worse than it would destroy a wedding dress.

Only this time, I was very eager for what would happen next. Your mom and I entered marriage as virgins, but we weren't perfectly pure. There were times during our dating relationship that we had kissed too long, touched too much, and went too far even though we stopped short of disrobing or having intercourse. Now, upon the cusp of receiving our reward for a job pretty well done, I felt a sense of shame and remorse. I wished I were entering the marriage bed for the first time with my beautiful dream bride with much less experience and much more purity. I had done too much with her already. I had seen way too much through pornography. Now, moments before I had sex for the first time ever, I regretted every previous impure thought and action.

Son, I would have loved to see you get married. Marriage is one of the greatest gifts God gives. I bet you would have been a good husband and married a great woman. I'm sorry you never got to experience this relationship. But in some ways, too, I am relieved you never had to fight the giant of lust in your heart. Jesus took you home before you had to engage that enemy. And for most men, the enemy lust and the fight for sexual purity is the defining war of their lives.

I miss you, Son. I like to think I wouldn't have officiated your wedding; I like to think I would have been your best man.

For Jesus' fame,
Dad

. . .

The first step in protecting your purity is to comprehend how God defines the term.

When Scripture discusses the qualifications for church leaders, it speaks frankly regarding marriages of prospective leaders. In three different places, the healthy state of marriage to be experienced by men who will lead the church is defined as "the husband of one wife" (1 Timothy 3:2, 12 and Titus 1:6). While not every man is called to be an elder or deacon in the church, every married man is called to be the "husband of one wife."

the husband of one wife
—1 Timothy 3:2

the husband of one wife
—1 Timothy 3:12

the husband of one wife
—Titus 1:6

There are some instances when we study the Bible that having a grasp of the original language of Scripture is superhelpful. As you likely know by now, the Bible wasn't first written in modern English. It was written in the ancient languages of Hebrew, Aramaic, and Koine Greek. Paul used Greek when he wrote to Pastor Timothy and Pastor Titus and the churches they served. The phrase translated in your Bible as "the husband of one wife" most literally is translated as "a one-woman man" in the original language. I love that rendering because I think it is most helpful.

A "one-woman man" better defines for me God's vision for my role as a husband. It doesn't mean I love only one woman at a time. It plainly means I love one woman for all of my life until "death do us part." This is what I pledged to Kara on that snowy December night twenty-five years ago. On that night, as we were about to consummate our marriage, I wished I had lived true to that pledge prior to our marriage as well. But this is the opportunity in front of you from this day forward: to be a one-woman man.

The marriage relationship is all about oneness: two people, a man and a woman, become one for life. Jesus said it best, as he always does. When questioned by religious men who were seeking to justify their perverted view of marriage, divorce, and remarriage, Jesus said, "Have you not read that he who created them from the beginning made them male and female, and said, 'Therefore a man shall leave his father and his mother and hold fast to his wife, and the two shall become one flesh'? So they are no longer two but one flesh. What therefore God has joined together, let not man separate" (Matthew 19:4-6).

Another way of understanding biblical oneness is through the word *intimacy*. Marriage is a unique relationship defined by a unique intimacy. You will experience intimacy spiritually, emotionally, and sexually with your wife in a way that is exclusively reserved for her. This is exactly what it means to be a one-woman man. You are committing to live in the power of the Holy Spirit as one flesh with one woman through the entirety of one life.

Today you have the opportunity to commit to one woman for life. Even if, and maybe especially if, you don't even know her today. Whether you are dating someone seriously, going out with a young woman for the first time, or just happily living the life of a bachelor without any romantic prospects, you always are preparing for marriage. The most important way to prepare for marital bliss tomorrow is to protect your purity today. This means you refuse to give yourself to a woman in any way that should be reserved solely for your wife. You will refuse to have spiritual, emotional, or sexual intimacy with any woman who doesn't share your last name. That covenant begins now!

This is the opportunity in front of you from this day forward: to be a one-woman man.

The biggest and most painful error I watch an unmarried young Christian man make is to relate to an unmarried young Christian woman today as if they will be married tomorrow and forever. This means he is jumping the gun on intimacy emotionally, spiritually, and sexually with a woman he may or may not someday marry. The devastating consequence is that both enter into marriage having prematurely experienced something that could have been so much more meaningful and rich and intimate had they patiently waited. Or worse yet, they eventually move on from their relationship and marry others having already given themselves away intimately to someone other than a spouse.

In this area, a proverbial good offense is the best defense. In the power of the Holy Spirit, you can guard your purity today in order to give it to your future wife tomorrow. You can do so by refusing to engage intimately with any woman other than your wife. Do this, and you will protect not only your purity but also that of your sisters in Christ who will someday marry your brothers. Do this well, and the whole body of Christ wins.

Our cultural view of personhood, in which we categorize individuals into complex and separate parts, compartmentalizes people in a manner that has devastating consequences. The Bible presents people in a far more integrated sense. Although the concept of sacred sexual intimacy between a husband and a wife is in serious decline, our culture still has some awareness of it—even if many disregard it. But society today certainly has no category for the emotional and spiritual intimacy that should exist only between married people. The result is a cultural view of dating and courtship that sets young people up for future disaster. Some of these dangerous views have seeped into Christian culture. Although all biblical Christians would hold the conviction that sexual intimacy has no place in a premarital relationship, they often naively and destructively permit (and often encourage) unmarried people to engage in emotional and spiritual intimacy that should be reserved for marriage. More often than not, emotional and spiritual intimacy before marriage leads to sexual intimacy before marriage.

Guard yourself emotionally as you relate to young women. It's good and healthy to have female friends. You should relate to women who don't know Jesus in a respectful and friendly manner. You should treat young women who know Jesus as sisters. But to give yourself completely and entirely to a woman you aren't married to is inappropriate and will be harmful to you both.

Married people all too often engage in what is referred to as an "emotional affair." In other words, a married man will give his affection and emotion away to a woman who is not his wife in a manner that should be exclusively reserved for his wife. If this is a real category—and I firmly believe it is—it's also possible for an unmarried man to give himself away to an unmarried woman emotionally in a manner that may not be categorically an "emotional affair," but would be better classified as "emotional promiscuity" or "premarital emotional intimacy." This is extremely dangerous.

Take Nick, for example. He was a handsome young man with a good job. But what was most impressive about Nick was his charm. He made everyone he knew feel important. And sadly, Nick left a trail of heartbroken young women in his path—women who were convinced that they would soon be Mrs. Nick and then were ditched for another potential bride as things got serious. But Nick's exes still thought he was great. Even though they were wrecked by him, they had the nicest things to say about him. He was a gentleman.

And they were very emotionally connected to him, which made losing his friendship even worse. And that was the very root of the problem: Nick had built emotional intimacy with many women yet never committed himself to them.

Having led a home for many years now where I live as a minority in a sorority (one man living with a wife and four daughters), I see more than ever that women are generally more emotionally complex than men. This also means young women may be more vulnerable to emotional manipulation than men. Sadly, I have watched men and women build emotionally intimate relationships that cause enormous devastation for the woman when the relationship breaks apart. These women feel used and discarded and broken.

Christina is someone I knew who was a very broken young woman. Her dad wasn't kind to her or protective of her. He used her: he would give her cash so that she would buy him drugs. That way, if she got caught, he wouldn't go to jail. But her dad wasn't the only man who used her. Christina was in and out of serious relationships constantly. She was emotionally needy, and far too many young men took advantage of this vulnerability. Every failed relationship led to massive disappointment and hurt for Christina. And she progressively grew lonelier.

There is such a thing as a healthy aloofness as you interact with women—even with the women you may choose to date. Always be kind, encouraging, and affirming. But be cautious in sharing from your wellspring of emotion. Such depths aren't to be plumbed until marriage. You will have a lifetime of sharing your feelings with the woman you are blessed to marry. I don't mean that you should be duplicitous or hide sin. But guard your heart by giving it away to one woman only.

You are also responsible before Jesus and the dad of the woman you date to guard her emotional intimacy. You set and maintain the boundaries. Tobin, my son-in-law, was very respectable and cautious with my daughter Lisa while they were dating. Most specifically, he avoided talking about marriage before it was an appropriate topic of conversation. This protected Lisa emotionally. She didn't think of herself as Tobin's potential wife prior to their formal engagement. Being "potentially married" puts enormous emotional pressure on a man and woman. But Tobin's leadership in maintaining emotional boundaries in their relationship allowed great security and growth for her.

It can be particularly tempting to cross over into emotional intimacy when a woman you care about is going through a hard time. She very well may want to pour out her heart to you and find comfort in you. Be wary! It's your job to protect those boundaries when she is emotionally vulnerable. Understand that as a potential husband, you aren't responsible for healing wounds or counseling through pain. There are mature women and pastors who can assist in that endeavor.

One of the big mistakes I made with my wife-to-be was leading us down a path of premature spiritual intimacy. I loved her very much as we dated and wanted to do everything I could to help her grow in her relationship with Jesus. (Don't get me wrong; it's not that her spiritual life was stunted. Since the day I met her, she has been the most dynamic Christian I have known.) But it is wise to set limits and boundaries here as well. If I had not married her, I would have felt guilty about how before we were married I led her in a manner that should be reserved for a husband.

We studied the Bible together, prayed together, went to church together, went on mission trips, and even attended camps and conferences together. There was something very good and encouraging about being together in a community on mission with Jesus. But there were other things that weren't as helpful. One-on-one prayer sessions in isolated places. Confrontation and counseling that should have been led by those in positions of spiritual authority over us. There were instances in which we both felt that we had crossed a line spiritually that should be reserved for marriage. Yet sadly, at least among our peers, this type of spiritual interaction was strongly encouraged and frequently practiced.

You must understand how physically attractive a spiritual person of the opposite gender can become to a spiritually minded person. I think that is one reason why so many pastors fall into sexual immorality. I believe—although I can't point to any specific verses, so this should be suspect—that spiritual intimacy accompanies physical intimacy. If that is so, then premature spiritual intimacy may very well lead to premarital sexual intimacy. Kara and I faced the strongest sexual temptation during our most spiritually intimate moments. When someone you are attracted to emotionally and physically nurtures the most important aspect of your existence—your relationship with Jesus—it is a very strong and consequential desire to give yourself to this person completely, including sexually. So you can do great preventative work against the sin of sexual immorality by setting and keeping, in the power of the Holy Spirit, spiritual-intimacy boundaries.

The best prevention against premature spiritual intimacy is family and church community. If the woman you are dating has a spiritually responsible dad, do everything you can to keep yourself and his daughter both under his leadership. You have no right whatsoever to take spiritual leadership over a Christian young woman until her Christian father gives it to you on your wedding day. Jesus, quoting some of the very first words of the Bible, says it this way: "'A man shall leave his father and his mother and hold fast to his wife, and the two shall become one flesh.' . . . So they are no longer two but one flesh" (Matthew 19:5-6). The biblical concept of family implied in this text is that men and women are grounded in their families of origin prior to marriage. Upon marriage, they begin a new family. God never intended for young men and young women to drift from the protection and blessing of familial structure, even if they live independent from home. Never forget that. Let that principle guide you, and you will do well during your courtship of God's precious daughter.

The simplest way to place yourself in the appropriate

spiritual leadership position with a woman's father is to know and respect him. Allow his voice to be the strongest and most authoritative that your girlfriend hears. Submit to him your plans for his daughter. Seek his counsel as you build a relationship with her. Keep him informed of your intentions. Ask him to pray for you as you get to know her.

If the woman you are interested in doesn't have a believing father or even a father at all, then seek together a trustworthy mature Christian to help you and hold you accountable. This is God's structure for family life. Violate it at your own potential peril.

We live in a sexually supercharged world. There are people who don't know Jesus, and many who do know him don't understand that sex is an act of worship. It's an act that's reserved solely for a man and woman living in the covenant of marriage.

But sexual purity with a view toward marriage for a single Christian man begins on the day of his conversion. Long before sex involves genitals, it is dormant in the hearts and souls of men and women. That's why Jesus said, "You have heard that it was said, 'You shall not commit adultery.' But I say to you that everyone who looks at a woman with lustful intent has already committed adultery with her in his heart" (Matthew 5:27-28). Take these words into consideration when you devise a strategy to guard your sexual purity. Rules concerning dating conduct, Internet filters, and accountability groups do very little to guard the heart.

In this sexual world, there is an unlimited stream of real

and cybersex partners waiting for you twenty-four hours a day, 365 days a year, at your fingertips. They can be easily reached on your desktop, laptop, or smartphone. You can have sex with them in your heart without anyone else knowing. This makes it very possible for you to live a double life—one in which you honor Jesus with your lips but your heart is far from him. This is what Jesus criticized most when he walked the earth. Mark 7:6 records his words: "Well did Isaiah prophesy of you hypocrites, as it is written, 'This people honors me with their lips, but their heart is far from me.'"

To make matters even more dangerous, you are living among peers who have spent time in this cyberworld long enough to start living out, with real people and partners, what they have seen played out through electronic imagery. Many of those peers live within the church community.

Please understand the progression of sin. What starts in the heart as lust eventually makes its way outwardly into your hands. Then it spills over into the lives of the real people you love. You most certainly will become whatever is in your heart. You will act upon your desires. That reality must frame your strategy for protecting your sexual purity as well as for safeguarding your sisters in Christ.

The pressing issue in your heart isn't so much about sex. It's actually about worship. Your heart was wired for worship. And when it comes to the issue of sex and your heart, there really are only two options: you either will worship the image of beautiful and sexually available women in your heart or you will worship the magnificent image of God found in the face of Jesus (see 2 Corinthians 4:6). The most surefire weapon you have to fight against the worship of sex and to fight for the worship of Jesus in your heart is the Word of God.

Psalm 119:9-11 asks the big question, then gives the best answer:

> How can a young man keep his way pure?
>   By guarding it according to your word.
> With my whole heart I seek you;
>   let me not wander from your commandments!
> I have stored up your word in my heart,
>   that I might not sin against you.

So you see, the way out of adultery in the heart is through worship. Heart worship is stimulated and fueled by a heart that is filled with Scripture. Ingesting God's Word at a heart level awakens a deep pleasure for his glory. His glory is far more pleasurable than the best porn ever made. Trust me; it is far more pleasurable than real sex.

I want you to be a one-woman man. Life really is very simple, despite the noise and chaos and complexity of our world. When your life comes to an end, you will want to be ready and prepared to meet Jesus. You will call the one woman you have loved all your life to your side. You will want to finish well. The path to finishing well begins with the single step of starting well. Today you begin being a one-woman man by the grace of God. Jesus will help you. You can be a one-woman man long before she ever shows up. Someday, she will thank you.

So What Now?

We talked earlier (in chapter 3) about the importance of treating women as sisters rather than as potential romantic partners. The Bible never affirms dating lots of different women until you find one you like; the biblical idea is to pursue one person for life. So how do you know when and whom to pursue? Two considerations are very important. First, let the Bible, then those in spiritual authority over you, both answer these two questions: "Is she a woman you could marry?" and "Are you a man she could marry?" Scripture gives permission for a believer to marry another believer provided that neither party is currently in another marriage covenant or still bound by a previous marriage covenant (see Matthew 5:31-32; 19:1-12; 1 Corinthians 7:39; 2 Corinthians 6:14-18). If you and the woman you are interested in meet those qualifications, and if godly leaders and friends encourage the relationship, then you have the freedom to move forward—with loving and supportive supervision and accountability.

The best context to get to know a woman you may consider dating is in the community of church. Worship together and serve together—in groups, to avoid the dangers of spiritual intimacy that we talked about earlier in this chapter. Learn as much as possible about her in a safe community context before you ask her out. Doing more work before starting a relationship to be sure a woman is someone you could marry potentially will spare both of you heartache later. Invite those you trust to speak wisdom into the possibility of courting a young woman. And never be shady about your intentions with others or with her. Speak the truth, and say it with love and respect.

While rules of engagement, Internet filters, and accountability partners are important once you are dating, nothing is more proactively deadly against the sin of lust that lives in our hearts than the internalizing of Scripture. So be in the Bible. Live in and live out the Word. Read it, study it, memorize it, and listen to it preached as often as possible. Be a part of a church that takes the Bible seriously. Ask the Holy Spirit to awaken your heart with worship for Jesus when you open up your Bible. And don't finish reading until your heart is on fire for him. You were created by God for pleasure. He has rewired you in Jesus to find the greatest pleasure in him. Don't settle for anything less.

Remember that sexual purity begins in the heart, moves toward the head, and ends up in your hands. Guard your heart. Rather than kill the passions in your heart, kindle them toward Jesus. Be careful with your mind. The images and thoughts you dwell on are important. The most sensitive and powerful sexual organ in your body is your brain, and you are bombarded with sexually oriented images on a daily basis. They may fall short of pornography, but some are just as deadly. Last, keep your hands pure. No one that I have met has ever regretted limiting physical contact with a young woman prior to marriage. Keep your hands off your sisters. Keep your hands off yourself. Jesus has something much better for you than you can even imagine today if you will patiently and diligently follow his plan, in his power.

One final thing we need to acknowledge: some men will be called to live lives fully devoted to Jesus apart from marriage. Jesus was a single man and lived the only perfect life that ever has been lived. And the apostle Paul encouraged single men and women to remain single if possible (see 1 Corinthians 7:8-9). This is a powerful life for those who have this calling. A man called to live a single life is free to focus more time and energy on worshiping Jesus and serving others than a husband and a dad who has family obligations.

What do you do if you worry that God is calling you to singleness (or to marriage) and you aren't happy about it? The book *Desiring God* by John Piper has deeply impacted my thinking on these things; I recommend it to you as well. I hope that reading it will assure you that whether Jesus calls you to be married or single, he does indeed have a good plan for those who love him. It's not always easy, but it is always worthwhile. He cares for you and has good things in store for you that will bring you fulfillment and him glory.

9
—
FATHER

Dear Son,

I was startled awake in the early morning hours of Good Friday in March 2008. There was a series of urgent knocks on the front door. I made my way to answer the door cautiously. We were living in a working-class neighborhood wedged in between the "War Zone" and Coronado Mall in Albuquerque, New Mexico. It seemed that property crime was an everyday occurrence. Violent crime showed up more on a monthly basis. Whatever was going on at my front door wasn't good and was overdue by my calculations. While it wasn't uncommon to be awakened in the middle of the night by a police helicopter flying overhead, an aggressive and unexpected knock at the door was unnerving.

I wasn't quite sure what to expect as I opened the door. But I was shocked to see the driver of a Dolly

Madison Bakery truck frantically knocking on my door while calmly speaking on his cell phone. His inconsistent body language confused me. As I opened the front door, but kept the screen door locked as a barrier between us, this man matter-of-factly pointed to an inferno blazing in my driveway and then mouthed the word *fire*. He was right. He finished his call to 911 and let me know the Albuquerque Fire Department was en route. I ran toward my two vehicles, a white Ford Explorer and a Chevy Suburban, to see if there was anything I could do to stop the flames. As I drew nearer, it became clear what had happened. Someone had taken shop-type cloth rags— the oily and thick kind you would see in a mechanic's garage—stuck them in the gas tank of each vehicle, and set them on fire.

As I uselessly tried to contain the fire, I got the sense that the cars were inevitably going to explode, like on TV, and the whole house would be engulfed in flames. The only instruction I had given Kara before I ran out the door was to shout, "Stay inside!" Now I worried that maybe I should have told her to grab the girls and run for safety. Fortunately, before there were any explosions, the fine members of the Albuquerque Fire Department arrived and quickly put out the blaze. The vehicles looked to be in rough shape, but the house was spared. Most important, Kara, Lisa, Lauren, Jennifer, and Jillian were safe inside. Other than Kara and Lisa, everyone else was still asleep. They wouldn't learn about what had happened until they woke up for breakfast.

The fire department officer informed me I could notify the police if I wished. But he also told me the police only would investigate if someone had been injured or property worth far more than two older and fully depreciated SUVs had been destroyed. When a kind officer from the Albuquerque Police Department showed up, she asked me only one question: "Who did you piss off?" I told her there were far too many people to remember, since that was my job as a preacher. She did leave me with these chilling words: "Sir, whoever did this is serious. They meant to hurt you and your family."

There were too many suspects swirling around my mind to count. Our church was reaching out to gang members, drug addicts, and otherwise everyday people who were afflicted with mental and emotional illnesses. Any one of them could have done this. I resolved to find out if possible. I was very thankful my family was safe. Things were headed back toward normal until I received a fateful phone call later that day.

The church I was pastoring at the time, City on a Hill, had just joined the Acts 29 Network. We did this so we could learn how to plant more churches. I texted Scott Thomas, the director of Acts 29 at the time, about the morning's events. He then informed Mark Driscoll, who was president of Acts 29 at the time. Within hours, flowers and candy had arrived for your mom and sisters as an expression of sympathy. Then a call came from an unrecognized number. The voice on the other end of the line was unmistakable. "Hey, buddy, this is Driscoll," said my friend. He asked a lot of questions about the incident. He asked even more questions about the well-being and safety of our family. I appreciated the call, especially knowing he had several Good Friday services to preach that night and too many to lead on Easter to count. He was very busy, and it was comforting to know he cared for my family and me. Then Mark left me with a haunting reminder before he hung up and ended the call: "Well, buddy, I'm sorry this happened. We love you and your family. And I just want to remind you that if you can't protect your family, you can't lead the church. Call me if you need anything."

Click.

I knew immediately he was right. My first calling wasn't to lead and serve the church but to love, lead, and serve my family. If my second calling to the church ever gets in the way of my first calling to my family, we have a problem. In some careless ways, I had put your mom and sisters in danger in order to reach people that still could be impacted if we lived in a safer place. While I do believe some men are called to such places, no one should put their kids in an unnecessary place of danger for the sake of ministry dreams and ideals, which is exactly what I had done. We had a family meeting. Within a few months, we relocated to a safer place and did more to protect our home.

David, if there is a haunting regret I have about your short life, it is the thought that as your dad I could have done more. Maybe I could have found a more renowned specialist with a different opinion. Maybe I should have transferred you to a different hospital. I just don't know. But nothing I have experienced feels worse than losing a son. I miss you so much. I want to believe I did everything I could do to save your life. On dark days, that is a little more difficult to hold on to. I look forward to our reunion. Maybe we can talk more about this then.

For Jesus' fame,

Dad

. . .

Becoming a dad is the best thing that can ever happen to a man, after becoming a Christian and a husband. Just as you can prepare to be a husband before you are married, you also can prepare to be a father before you have kids of your own. But to prepare for such a role, you must know its functions.

I'm thankful that Paul told Pastor Timothy what to look for in a father who is called to be a leader in the church. Through his instructions, we get a vision for healthy father-hood. Paul writes in 1 Timothy 3:4-5, "He must manage his own household well, with all dignity keeping his children submissive, for if someone does not know how to manage his own household, how will he care for God's church?" This is an interesting thought: a good pastor leads his church in the very same way a good dad leads his home, and a good dad leads his home in the very same way a good pastor leads his church. Do you see the logical connection here? If this is true—which I am quite certain it is—it gives us some categories we can work with as you prepare to be a dad someday.

Pastoral ministry consists of three big functions: preaching the gospel, presenting a good model for others to imitate, and protecting the church from doctrinal error and dangerous leaders. So if a dad were to function in his home as a pastor does within a church family, he would see his primary responsibilities as preacher, role model, and protector.

He must manage his own household well, with all dignity keeping his children submissive, for if someone does not know how to manage his own household, how will he care for God's church?

—1 Timothy 3:4-5

First let's look at a father's role as a preacher. While the pastor of a church should be well educated, whether formally or informally, so as to be an expert in the Bible, a good dad need not be an accomplished theologian. Although he should take advantage of every opportunity he is afforded to grow in his understanding of biblical truth so he can serve his family best, even without specialized training he will do well both to internalize and then communicate the gospel. Too many dads are more focused on their need for training than on trusting in the power of the gospel in the hands of the Holy Spirit to shape their homes.

This means a dad should be competent, with the help of a solid children's Bible, like *The Jesus Storybook Bible*, to read and explain the basic message of the Bible. "Jesus saves sinners" is the most important message for little ears to hear and little hearts to receive. Children and adults should never graduate from that message.

The biggest mistake I see dads make in pastoring their children is to tell them God loves good little boys and girls. Children are exhorted to be good so that God will love them. Yet this is a devastating distortion of the Bible. Nothing could be further from what the Bible has to say about kids or about God. The Bible teaches us that God loves bad little boys and girls through Jesus and helps them grow into children who obey him through the gift of the Holy Spirit.

I can't begin to count how many young men and women I know who have grown up in Christian homes where the Bible was taught and yet have never heard the good news of Jesus' righteousness available to them through faith. When they do hear the gospel clearly preached the first time, they respond by angrily asking, "Why have I never heard this before?" They were taught the Bible, but they weren't helped by it. Dad only taught them the rules of the Bible apart from Jesus. Despite Dad's best efforts, he totally missed the main point of Scripture. Perhaps he gets an A for effort, but he gets a big fat F as a pastor to his kids.

Prepare today for a lifetime of teaching the Bible to your

children. Study it for yourself. Listen to as many good sermons as you can get your ears on. Look for Jesus to be the hero in every Bible story. Discover for yourself how to grow in holiness through repentance and faith in the power of the Holy Spirit rather than through your own best efforts. Rules apart from Jesus equal mere religion.

Find a young dad you respect and ask him if you can observe him while he leads his family in the Bible. There are some things you can learn only by observing others in action. I believe teaching kids the gospel is one of those things. Then ask to serve by teaching children in your church. You will gain so much insight into the basic message of Scripture by teaching kids. You will get a great head start on being an effective pastor-dad when your day comes.

Remember, the best gospel lessons you will give to your children most likely will not be after dinner during formal family devotional time but will happen through object lessons in everyday life. This is why the Bible instructs dads in Deuteronomy 6:5-7 this way: "You shall love the LORD your God with all your heart and with all your soul and with all your might. And these words that I command you today shall be on your heart. You shall teach them diligently to your children, and shall talk of them when you sit in your house, and when you walk by the way, and when you lie down, and when you rise."

One thing I have learned over the years as a preacher is that you don't have to have a scheduled upcoming sermon to prepare a good message. Good sermons should be prepared regardless of when you will be preaching next. You can start preparing your lessons for your future family today. Journal the examples of Jesus at work in your life so that you can pass them on to your wife and children someday. They will find your life lessons much more interesting and helpful than you did. Remember, Jesus is preparing you today to be a dad tomorrow.

I believe the most important thing to do for your kids, next to preaching the gospel to them as their beloved pastor-dad, is to demonstrate what it looks like to respond to the gospel. In this way, you model how to apply the truths you teach. You also show them what it *doesn't* look like to be a growing Christian: you get to demonstrate for them the enormous difference between a living faith empowered by the Spirit and dead works linked to the flesh. As was the case in the early church, far too many Christians hear the good news of forgiveness and freedom through Jesus and respond to it wrongly by religiously doing more and trying harder to change in their own strength. You have a huge responsibility to show your sons and daughters what it is and what it isn't to live life in the power of the Holy Spirit.

A dad should see his primary roles as preacher, role model, and protector.

I have discovered a common theme among many young prodigals who have returned to Jesus after abandoning the convictions of their childhood: their dads were hypocrites. Often through tears, these young men and women tell the heartbreaking story of being led by a father to a faith he all too often denied in his own life. Most painfully, Dad never repented of obvious sin in front of his wife and children. He never said he was wrong or sorry. He never confessed his rebellion. He never spoke openly about needing Jesus' forgiveness for his personal sin against his family. He certainly never asked Mom or son or daughter to forgive him.

These young adults wrongly concluded, to their own detriment, that Dad's faith was no different from his view of Santa Claus: a myth to be talked about but lacking true impact in life transformation. Yet a very real and merciful Jesus had brought them home to himself.

As a dad who models a vibrant Christian faith for his children, nothing is more important than regularly and authentically repenting of your own sin—especially when your sin has hurt your children or their mother. When you, with a broken heart, acknowledge your own sin and your own need for Jesus' forgiveness, you are fighting the internal default mechanism toward religiosity. You are doing so with the greatest weapon at your disposal: the humility that comes from desperately needing the grace of God through Jesus again. Never manipulate your family with this strategy. But use it as often as it is available, which should be at least once every day, and you will find that your children will pay closer attention to your words and actions.

A dad who leads his family well will never be perfect. But he will be progressing toward being a man who thinks, feels, speaks, and acts like Jesus through the power of the

Holy Spirit. Whether today or in the distant future, his dear children will take note. They, too, will understand that Jesus forgives sinners. They will get that Jesus frees sinners to live lives of worship. They will see firsthand from Dad's example that Jesus fills sinners with the Holy Spirit as the greatest gift available in his assortment of grace-gifts.

A pastor must protect his flock from false teaching and predatory leaders. So you must do the same with your little flock, your family. At the heart of every rebellious act your kids will commit is a false belief. They will deny the gospel through their treason against the God who loves them in Jesus. They will disappoint you and your wife with their mutiny. But you must understand that all sin in thought, word, attitude, and action has root in denying healthy doctrine or believing false doctrine. This means you can head off the future heartache of sin by confronting false teaching proactively.

I'm amazed by how many false messages children hear daily from friends, other adults, and media. Even the most wholesome music, television shows, and movies often are laden with false doctrine. You, as a father, will be faced with a couple of options. You either can prevent your children from hearing and seeing content that doesn't sync with the Bible, or you can allow them to see and hear things that provide opportunities to learn so they may grow to identify what is wrong and learn to be discerning.

I believe you must protect your children from ideas that will hurt them if embraced, especially when your children aren't emotionally, mentally, or physically mature enough to deal with such contradictions. As your kids mature, I believe in allowing content that isn't intrinsically evil and damaging to be evaluated for the sake of reinforcing true and healthy doctrine. Viewing a film that has some non-Christian themes with a finger on the pause button is a very effective way to help kids see the difference between truth and error and the resulting consequences.

You also must be vigilant in guarding who has relational access to your children. Adults, youth, and other children who are family and friends most frequently do far more hurtful damage to children than music, TV shows, or movies. This makes the selection of your church home extremely important. Choose a church that preaches doctrine according to your convictions. Then you will find that the friends you meet through church will reinforce what you want your children to embrace.

The only thing more destructive to your children's faith than false doctrines will be other Christians who either hold to false doctrine or who don't live faithfully in light of the gospel of Jesus. I have found that this second category of people do far more damage to my efforts to pastor my children than non-Christians who openly disbelieve in Jesus. Accordingly, that is why the Bible implores us to disassociate with Christians living openly and unrepentantly in regards to error or sin. (It also instructs us not to do the same with unbelievers living in sin [see 1 Corinthians 5:9-13].) Again, you will do well to choose a church that takes these truths seriously. Pick a church that graciously practices church discipline, dealing lovingly but firmly with Christians who are living in unrepentant sin.

The best thing you can do today in order to protect your children tomorrow is to be a good student of the Bible and culture. Follow the advice of Jesus to his very first followers as he sent them into a hostile world: "I am sending you out as sheep in the midst of wolves, so be wise as serpents and innocent as doves" (Matthew 10:16). I have grown weary of meeting young Christian men who have this text reversed:

> The best thing you can do today in order to protect your children tomorrow is to be a good student of the Bible and culture.

they are as innocent as serpents and as wise as doves. They will be leading their future families to the slaughter as sheep amongst ferocious and hungry wolves.

Finally, let's look at the role of provider. How impotent would a pastor be if he didn't believe the gospel? That is exactly the position of a pastor-dad who is unable to provide financially for his family. We considered this in chapter 5, but it's worth looking at again. I want you to take this text with all the importance it demands: "If anyone does not provide for his relatives, and especially for members of his household, he has denied the faith and is worse than an unbeliever" (1 Timothy 5:8). While this thought is plenty daunting, it also has the ability to motivate you today with tomorrow in view. You can be a future provider for your wife and children right here and right now. Work hard. Work smart. Be a good steward. Do it all as an act of faith, trusting in the power of the Holy Spirit to help you. Jesus will be pleased. Your future family will be blessed. You will have great joy when the day comes that you have the enormous privilege of being a provider.

So What Now?

Begin preparing today for this heavy responsibility you will have tomorrow. Grow in your knowledge and understanding of Scripture so that you can both teach it and live it. Invite others to look into your life today. Find dads with young children who are doing a good job and seek out their help. Practice repentance each and every day in front of others so you aren't just trying it on for size when your family shows up. Work hard so that you can be a good provider one day.

Being a dad is what you have been created to be. God told our first parents, Adam and Eve, "Be fruitful and multiply and fill the earth" (Genesis 1:28)—the very first mission statement in the Bible. But sin entered the world and will cause you to resist this calling. The good news is that Jesus has overcome your sin. Trust him, and he will redeem fatherhood for you the way he has for my dad and me. You will be continuing the legacy of faith for your kids too. Few things in life will bring you more joy than seeing your children love and worship Jesus. With Jesus' help, work toward that happy and fulfilling future today. If you are married, have children. And if you are unable to have biological children, consider adoption. Your heart will be enlarged for your kids and toward God as you begin to experience the love a father has for his children.

10
—
VESSEL

Dear Son,

Both of your grandfathers are remarkable men. Any man would do well to love Jesus, lead his family, and serve the church in the manner they have. Recently, Grandpa Dale—your mom's dad—had his second kidney removed to save his life from cancer. This means he has to maintain a rigorous dialysis schedule. Every Tuesday, Thursday, and Saturday, he must drive an hour-and-a-half round-trip to undergo four hours of treatment in a regional medical center. He rarely feels energetic or strong. He's had to hire help in order to keep his ranch in Texas operational.

I recently learned that his favorite day of the week is Sunday. Not because it's his designated day of much-deserved rest. He actually works very hard on Sundays, but not on his ranch. Rather, it is his

favorite day because it is the day he gets to be a part
of the church. He has continued to serve actively as
a deacon. He teaches a Bible class on Sundays. He
preaches occasionally to give the pastor a vacation
break. Each and every Sunday, he's together with the
people Jesus loves most doing what Grandpa does
best. He encourages and prays for everyone who will
allow him to do so. He loves serving the church, so he
loves Sundays.

Grandaddy—my dad—loves and serves the church
faithfully too. As a volunteer, he takes care of the
church facility that regularly hosts one thousand
men, women, youth, and children on Sundays. He
also serves as a greeter when there are services.
Guests love him, and many return just because
Grandaddy has welcomed them so warmly. I've had
many people tell me that the way he spoke to them
made them instantly feel loved and know there
was something far more to the people who were
gathering than typical "religious" convictions. They
have told me they felt the presence of Jesus among
the people who meet there.

Both of your grandfathers have loved and served
the church well for decades. As a pastor who makes a
livelihood by serving and leading the church, I see these
men, and other men like them, as heroes. I deeply
respect their sacrifice in serving others faithfully
without the incentive of a paycheck. I'm convinced they

will receive a great reward when Jesus gives gifts to those who have faithfully served his people.

I wish you could know these fine men. If you were still with us, nothing would make me prouder than to see you continuing this legacy of loving, serving, and leading others in Jesus' church as a volunteer.

For Jesus' fame,

Dad

. . .

Many Christians falsely believe that the apex of faith is being a vocational pastor or deacon or missionary. While there may have been a time and age when that was the case, I'm now convinced that the best thing a young man can do both to serve the church and to impact those in his generation who don't yet know Jesus is to work in the secular marketplace while being a faithful member of a church. That's how you can be useful to Jesus as he continues his mission through his Spirit-empowered people, the church.

Paul's words to Pastor Timothy are not exclusively for men in paid pastoral ministry. Paul tells young Timothy, "In a great house there are not only vessels of gold and silver but also of wood and clay, some for honorable use, some for dishonorable. Therefore, if anyone cleanses himself from what is dishonorable, he will be a vessel for honorable use, set apart as holy, useful to the master of the house, ready for every good work" (2 Timothy 2:20-21). This passage has many important truths to unpack. But none is more significant than the biggest idea in this text: if you wish to be useful to Jesus in his church, you should pursue personal holiness.

If you wish to be useful to Jesus in his church, you should pursue personal holiness.

Two actions are prescribed here. First, to be used best by Jesus like a reliable vessel, you must cleanse yourself from what is dishonorable or sinful. According to the Bible, God cleanses us from sin as Christians through confession (see 1 John 1:6-10). The act of confession is simply agreeing with God about his offense at your sin.

Second, you put on the holiness of Jesus by faith. This means your holiness isn't intrinsic or dormant within you. It is an external holiness that comes from Jesus and is gifted to you. You put on, or apply, his holiness—being set apart for God—by your trust in his reliability. These two acts, turning away from sin and turning again toward Jesus, are called repentance. Repentance from sin results in holiness. Practical and personal holiness renders you most effective in the hands of Jesus for the service of his people on his mission.

We live in a secular culture that is impressed most with talent, skill, and competency. This culture has seeped like runaway sewage into the foundation of the church. But your usefulness to Jesus and your fruitfulness in the church will be determined far more by your character than by your competency. So work to improve upon the skills needed to better serve the people loved by Jesus. Don't neglect developing your skills, but work even harder, by faith, to grow into a man who reflects the character of Jesus. You become a man who feels, thinks, speaks, and acts like Jesus only through repenting of sin. Do it in the empowerment of the Holy Spirit. As you become like Jesus, you will better serve the church—because no one has ever served the church better than Jesus.

You have been gifted by God so you may serve others. Paul reminds Timothy "to fan into flame the gift of God, which is in you through the laying on of my hands, for God gave us a spirit not of fear but of power and love and self-control" (2 Timothy 1:6-7). God's gifts aren't limited to those who work for the church in exchange for money. Nor are they reserved only for those with official titles. His gifts are for everyone who knows Jesus, so that everyone who belongs to him grows into full maturity. As you serve the church through your God-given gift(s), here are two very important reminders from this text.

First, the gift belongs to God, not to you. That's why Paul doesn't reveal what Timothy's gift is but rather to whom his gift belongs. According to Paul, it is a "gift of God." Your giftedness is to be seen not as belonging to you but to God. It is solely for the use of serving his people. It was never meant for your edification or self-worth. If you don't

> *If anyone cleanses himself from what is dishonorable, he will be a vessel for honorable use, set apart as holy, useful to the master of the house, ready for every good work.*
> —2 Timothy 2:21

175

get this basic concept, you will move from church to church and role to role trying to find the best fit so you may use "your" gift most effectively. The sooner you realize the gift you exercise belongs to God, and he has gifted it to you for the benefit of others, the more apt you will be to exercise it as an act of worship toward him for the service of his church. The selfish impulse to showcase your gift to your own glory will be overcome by a new and godly desire to be a gift to others in the church for his glory.

Second, much like young Timothy, you will face the temptation to fearfully hide your gift rather than to exercise it. I have met many young men who come to church to selfishly and timidly consume. Far too many pastors consider young men notoriously unreliable and uncommitted to the local church. Statistically speaking, young men are the least likely candidates to attend, much less serve in, the church. If they do attend church, they often will move from church to church in gangs like parasites sucking life from the body. According to Paul's words, they are driven by fear. Fear leads inevitably to impotent selfishness along with a lack of control. But God wants you to be a contributor rather than a consumer in his family. Making a contribution will require the power of the Holy Spirit, who enables a bold and serving love expressed in self-control.

The best way to discover your gift is to jump in and serve in community. Get busy and help out where you find unmet needs. Jesus is amazingly efficient in showing us our gifts through the needs of his community, the church. Then, while working hard to serve others, humbly and patiently look for fruitfulness. Seek input from others. They can affirm your gifts or gently redirect you toward more productive areas of service.

While Scripture does give us quite a few categories of gifts to consider (see 1 Corinthians 12 and Romans 12), it's best to first look at the two broadest categories of gifts: speaking gifts and serving gifts (see 1 Peter 4:10-11). In other words, ask yourself, *Do I best serve others through my words or through my works?* My father-in-law is gifted with using his words to help others. My father serves best through his works. Both men are supernaturally gifted, and others benefit tremendously as they are cared for and served by these men.

The needs of Jesus' family are constantly in flux. So don't get accustomed to a job description as you serve. That is the wonderful thing about being a servant. Your master, Jesus, will determine what you do, who you do it for, and when you do it. He will use those in spiritual authority over you to help you see what you can best do to serve. While such men are never infallible or perfectly reliable, Jesus is. He can perfectly use imperfect leaders in the church to achieve his highest and most redemptive purposes. Trust him first. He is sovereign as he rules over every providentially determined detail. He is good, too, always working to conform his people to his likeness. As you trust him more to place you

Ask yourself, Do I best serve others through my words or through my works?

in his church, you will be able to trust those who exercise the highest human authority in the church.

Paul tells Timothy, "The saying is trustworthy: If anyone aspires to the office of overseer, he desires a noble task" (1 Timothy 3:1). Do you aspire to this noble task? Jesus will be pleased if you wish to serve in the most sacrificial way. If you are called to do so, nothing is more sacrificial than being a volunteer elder in the local church. Men who desire this from pure hearts are to be commended and honored.

Some men look to the church for employment. This, for them, seems to trump serving the church. In other words, if they can't serve the church they attend vocationally, they look elsewhere until they find a church that will hire them— sometimes even at the cost of providing for their families. Or they stay way too long in an unpaid internship at the expense of their future family's finances. Some of these young Christian men, if they can't find a church to hire them, just start their own church in hopes of cultivating a livelihood for themselves someday. This is a terrible way to plant a church.

As one who has given much of his life to planting churches and preparing future church planters, I am concerned there are too many church plants happening today. I realize that is a shocking thing to write and may cause others to push back, so let me explain myself better.

America doesn't simply need more churches. We need more *healthy* churches. At the heart of a healthy church is a pastor who preaches "not in plausible words of wisdom, but in demonstration of the Spirit and of power, so that your faith might not rest in the wisdom of men but in the power of God" (1 Corinthians 2:4-5). A preacher like this preaches "Jesus Christ and him crucified" (1 Corinthians 2:2) in a manner in which hearts are persuaded and faith is granted. Through this type of preaching, non-Christians become Christians, and Christians become more like Jesus. These results are what is meant by the "demonstration of the Spirit and of power."

There are way too many churches where preaching like this is missing. Usually it is due to one of two possibilities. Either the true gospel isn't the central message or, quite possibly, Jesus Christ is preached without power. I personally have visited many churches led by preachers who can't preach in a manner that demonstrates the power of the Holy Spirit. Few, if any, of their listeners are ever converted. Believers don't seem to be transformed. The church is bearing very little fruit because the preaching isn't fruitful.

Some of these churches are led by young men who planted their church as a means of introducing new philosophies of ministry to reach non-Christians. Others started churches that are committed to caring more deeply for Christians than existing churches do. Despite the best intentions of these young church planters and pastors, without transformational, Jesus-centered preaching at the core, these churches just absorb precious resources while existing churches are diluted and opportunities for broader cultural influence are lost.

If you are called to plant a church, I would heartily

encourage you—provided that two things are confirmed by biblically qualified leaders from a healthy sponsoring church. First, you must have a confirmed call to *preach*. You must have demonstrated preaching with power in the past. There must be more than potential and good intentions on your résumé. This also means there must be verified cases of people who have been converted and/or transformed through the Holy Spirit working through you as you've preached. Second, you must have a confirmed call to *plant*. The gift of preaching isn't in itself enough to warrant a church plant. But when a sending church feels compelled to endorse a gifted preacher devoted to starting a new church for the sake of new people meeting Jesus, the preacher is well on his way to being legitimate.

I've painfully watched too many new churches launched in reaction to existing churches. These new churches are, in many respects, the antichurch of the church from which the core of the new church has emerged. They are, in their own perspective, more relevant, more loving, more true, more committed, more contextualized, more everything, ad nauseam, than the churches they have left. More often than not, they are led by ambitious young men who will learn eventually and painfully that there is a right way and a wrong way to plant a church. They will also learn that while you can grow a church by proclaiming what you are against, you can't grow a healthy church by doing so. I would be so disappointed if you planted a church like this. I would be just as disappointed if you joined a church like this.

So What Now?

My greatest desire for you is to join a healthy church, then serve that church humbly and faithfully. Much like the commitment you will someday make to your wife, you should serve the church for better or for worse, for richer, for poorer, in sickness and in health. Be patient and work through conflict.

If you haven't done so before, I strongly encourage you to approach the leaders in your church and ask them humbly, "What can I do to serve?" Trust Jesus to guide them as he reveals to you your place of service in his family. The church never was meant to be a place where you showcase your gifts. It always was meant to be a place where Jesus' fame and greatness are revealed by his gift to his people in being well cared for by one another. When the day is done, it is far more important that you have served others in need than that the gift you have been given has been perfectly utilized and admired. Far too many have disconnected from the body in missing this point, and it's very tragic. It means both the disconnected member and the dismembered body are worse off as a result.

Those who make the greatest impact serving others are those who serve for long seasons. Be a vessel of honor used mightily by Jesus. Know that he most powerfully uses the most ordinary vessels marked by extraordinary holiness. Be like my father and father-in-law. For great is their reward.

11

MORTAL

Dear Son,

As a pastor, I have been trusted by quite a few people to spend their very last few minutes of life with them and their loved ones. I have been alongside many deathbeds. I have also been with grieving families while death is still fresh. I have even had the very painful honor of notifying family members that loved ones have passed. But one passing stands out among the others. It was the death of my grandmother, "GG."

GG was the first Christian in her family. She prayed her daughters, sons-in-law, and grand-children would all meet Jesus. One by one, each member of GG's family came to know him. She was the spiritual matriarch of the family. She prayed for you, too, David. She held you in her arms before you died.

GG was diagnosed with liver cancer and given six to nine months to live. She lived only four months after her cancer was detected. I spent as much time with her as possible during her last days. I asked her many questions about life, family, faith, and death. As always, she gave me honest and serious answers. I remember asking her one day early in her struggle against cancer if she was afraid to die. She responded simply, "Of course I am. Wouldn't you be?" She reached over, took my hand, squeezed it hard as if to reprimand me for asking a question with such an obvious and uncomfortable answer. Then she smiled at me to remind me she loved me. I loved her, too, very much. Few people, if any, have had more impact on who I am today as a Christian, husband, and father. I made a private vow in that moment to be with GG while she died so she wouldn't be so afraid. I prayed Jesus would give me that privilege, and he graciously granted my request.

GG was in hospice in the neighborhood hospital during the last days of her life. She was mostly in a drug-induced fog. She was seldom coherent. The family would take turns sleeping in the extra bed next to her so that when her time came, she wouldn't die alone. One night I awoke to see her trying to pluck imaginary butterflies from the air. She would giggle and call out to her mama and papa when she caught one she thought was exceptionally pretty. It was as if during her last days on earth, confined to a bed in hospice, she went back to her first days of childhood memory in Louisiana. I thought that, in itself, was a gift of mercy to her from the Jesus who had loved her through good and hard times all her life.

Then, one day soon after, with her family gathered around, her labored breathing became erratic. It was clear she was passing. I put my ear to her chest and listened to her irregular heartbeat stop altogether. I waited for a few long moments. I thought she might recover, but she was gone to be with Jesus forever. As I left her hospice room for the last time, I was struck by how full, purposeful, and fruitful her life had been. She died surrounded by those she loved most, and she was in good standing with the Jesus she worshiped. Son, GG wasn't perfect. Actually, she was far from it. By her own admission, she had wasted many years as a younger woman. But she finished well and enjoyed seeing all her big prayer requests answered by the God who saved her, then took her home. GG not only taught me how to die well in that sacred moment of her passing; more important, she also instructed me how to live well.

For Jesus' fame,
Dad

. . .

I know it's not a popular topic of conversation, but it's important to remember that someday, we all will die. Young men don't often think about their dying days, but everyone's day will come, and it's a sober reminder to be busy with God's will, not chasing after youthful pleasures in life. If you live each day with the end of your life in view, you will not only finish well but also will start adult life well and live purposefully at every place between the two points.

Last words have been said to be lasting words. The following may have been the very last words written or spoken from sonless Paul to fatherless Timothy: "I am already being poured out as a drink offering, and the time of my departure has come. I have fought the good fight, I have finished the race, I have kept the faith. Henceforth there is laid up for me the crown of righteousness, which the Lord, the righteous judge, will award to me on that Day, and not only to me but also to all who have loved his appearing" (2 Timothy 4:6-8). Although we don't have much historical record, tradition informs us that Paul was beheaded by Nero within years of writing these words. Perhaps Timothy made it to visit his spiritual father one more time as Paul requested: "Do your best to come before winter" (2 Timothy 4:21). Maybe he didn't. It's largely conjecture, and maybe some wishful thinking, but I would like to believe Paul's words about finishing well guided Timothy through the rest of his life here on earth.

Like all men who ever have lived, you will someday die. Jesus is waiting for you beyond this world. Then life's most important questions will be those Paul confidently answers in this text: Did you fight the good fight, did you finish the race, did you keep the faith? Answer these questions with a resounding yes, and you will have lived a life filled with worship, service, joy, and meaning. Answer these questions with no, and all you have pursued and accomplished will be absolutely empty and meaningless.

Let's look deeply into Paul's words and see his life strategy. First, he lived to please God through Jesus. Second, he held nothing back in this cause. Third, he was motivated by the reality that great reward awaited him. The danger in being young is thinking you will have time to consider an endgame strategy in later life. This would be a huge mistake. Statistically speaking, you are safe in thinking you will have a long life with many years in front of you. But even if you do, you would be foolish to think who you are today doesn't make a difference in

I am already being poured out as a drink offering, and the time of my departure has come. I have fought the good fight, I have finished the race, I have kept the faith. Henceforth there is laid up for me the crown of righteousness, which the Lord, the righteous judge, will award to me on that Day, and not only to me but also to all who have loved his appearing.

—2 Timothy 4:6-8

who you will be tomorrow. You would be like a runner who is slow out of the blocks, then meanders in the first half of his marathon race. He will perhaps finish the race, but he won't win any prizes. Or you would be like a fighter who drops his guard in early rounds and allows his enemy to land heavy punches to his head. You would be just as foolish to live today without the final day in view.

I love Paul's metaphor of his life being like a drink offering. The drink offering is described in Numbers 28. Burnt offerings were made daily to the Lord at the Tabernacle, and later at the Temple. Accompanying those sacrifices were drink offerings that were poured out. Their primary purpose wasn't the atonement for sin. They were regular offerings made for the pleasure of God. This is the way you must view your Christian life.

Jesus has fully atoned for your sin. You are completely righteous in him. There is nothing you can add or subtract from the totality of his finished work. But you certainly can choose whether or not to live in his righteousness every day of your life. Paul saw his existence after he met Jesus as living to please God. Every thought, every affection, every attitude, every word, and every action was an opportunity to bring pleasure to God his Savior in worship through living the life of Jesus in the power of the Holy Spirit. If you take this same approach, your life will be radically different, tremendously purposeful, and incredibly powerful. Live to please God in everything. But don't do this so he will love you. Instead, do it boldly, knowing that he already does love you. See everything you do as an opportunity to worship Jesus. See everything you do as an opportunity to serve others. God, who is already pleased with you, will certainly be glorified in you.

Asking, then answering, the simple question *What will most please Jesus?* in all your decision making will lead you to say at your life's end, as Paul did, that you have been a "drink offering." Most young men don't ask themselves questions. Even fewer ask themselves good questions. This question is the best one you could ever ask yourself. Ask it often. Answer it as a man informed by the Scriptures. Ask other Christian men to help you with your answers. Make sure you are answering correctly. Then ask them to hold you accountable to living out the right answers.

I love Paul's language of being completely poured out in pleasing God. While this certainly means his cup of time on earth is now empty, with no more to be added, it may also mean he has left nothing in the chalice for himself or other pursuits outside of the pleasure of God. Please, leave nothing in your tank when it comes to pleasing God. Understand that your efforts must be empowered by his grace through his Spirit. But equally understand that pleasing God will drain every ounce of energy you have emotionally, spiritually, and physically. That's not bad news. Nothing will be more personally satisfying than giving your very best for God's greatest glory.

Most young men, from my limited perspective, hold back in going for it when it comes to pleasing Jesus—mainly, I think, because they are compromised by fear and pride.

They don't seem to understand yet how completely loved they are by God through Jesus. His big love for them liberates them from shame, guilt, and embarrassment. They are free to dream big and act big and even fail big for his glory.

I have a few regrets in my life. One of the bigger ones was passing up the opportunity to play college football. A few months before I headed out of state to attend college with the aid of a small academic scholarship, an assistant football coach called me. He told me he had seen film of my high school games. He let me know that he thought I could help the team, and he invited me to join as a walk-on. I was flattered. But I turned him down. Honestly, I was fearful I would fail. I was concerned about how it would look if I had to return to my hometown university and hang out with all my high school friends who were proud of my out-of-state opportunity. More than being worried about letting them down, I was caught up with not wanting to look like a failure. That's the pride I'm talking about. So in the end, I played it safe and stayed off the field.

I have personally found that both pride and fear of failure in the face of possible rejection have hindered me so many times in acting upon the answer to the question *What would most please Jesus?* The result is that I have left some of the drink offering in the cup over the years. I don't want you to make this same mistake. I want you to come to the end of your life with an empty cup, a cup that has been fully poured out for the pleasure of God. The only way you can be certain you will end your life poured out is to prepare now by making sure your cup is empty at the end of each day. All your energy spent in worshiping Jesus and serving people will never be wasted. Trust him to make the most of it. Be patient and persistent. He will pour more into your cup as you move forward with each new day. Trust him. He never lacks for resources.

As Paul comes to the end of his life spent pleasing God, he is motivated by the reward that awaits him. We should be too. I think far too often we believe that the Bible makes empty promises about future rewards for those who are faithful. Or we live in false humility by thinking it would be greedy to use this life to stack up rewards for the life to come. But we must live by faith. According to the most clear and basic definition of faith given to us in the Bible, "Without faith it is impossible to please him, for whoever would draw near to God must believe that he exists and that he rewards those who seek him" (Hebrews 11:6).

The only way you can be certain you will end your life poured out is to prepare now by making sure your cup is empty at the end of each day.

Few young Christian men struggle with the first half of biblical faith. Most see the existence of God through his creation and his goodness in providing for our most basic needs. But many young Christian men don't believe—or at least don't live as if they believe—that God rewards those who seek him. Paul did, and he wanted his spiritual son Timothy to do so also.

You have an amazing opportunity right in front of you today. You can live in this world, which is rapidly passing away, with another world that will last forever in view. Practically speaking, this means you can use the things you can't keep to gain things you can't lose. Live with perspective. Live your life in pursuit of the things that will last forever: God, his Word, his people, and his rewards. If you will do this, you will find yourself making consistent, values-based decisions. You will begin to thrive as you choose what is God's best rather than settle for what is just good. (Therein lies the greatest challenge in making choices. The temptation won't always involve having to choose between what is good and what is evil. But you must daily choose what is best over what is merely good.)

I think the two other metaphors the apostle Paul uses in describing his life are very helpful to us. They are both athletic images. Life is very much like running an endurance race; life is very much like fighting a mixed martial arts match. As a young man, you are in the beginning stages of each of these events.

Your life is marked out in front of you like a marathon. And marathons are grueling. Only those who run with discipline and determination finish. The secret of finishing well, according to Paul, is keeping the faith. When Paul uses the phrase "the faith," he is usually speaking about the basic doctrines that undergird our beliefs.

The only way to run with endurance the race set in front of you so you finish well is to live in and live out God's Word.

An endurance race has a way of getting in the runner's head. Long races are physically exhausting, but elite runners will tell you the true challenge is mental. A marathon can be very disorienting and confusing. With fatigue and a loss of perspective come the high likelihood that you will drift off course. A strong finish is most likely if you don't waste precious energy during the run by losing your way. Successful runners don't drift on and off the course.

As you run the marathon that is this life, two things will be a great drain on your energy and cause you to be ineffective: doubt and religious works. Doubt will result in your losing touch with Jesus' commitment to strengthen you as you run. You run in his power, which is made available to you in the enabling presence of the Holy Spirit. The Holy Spirit's available power is activated by your faith.

Religious works aimed at winning back the lost love of God will hinder your endurance more than anything else. You will sin as you run the race of life. You will blow it big-time. You most certainly will grieve the heart of God. You certainly will injure and offend those you love most. You will experience appropriate yet exhausting guilt, and guilt can ruin a good race.

What will you do when you sin? Will you do penance or repentance? Penance is about paying for your sin through your own work and suffering. Repentance is turning from sin and trusting that Jesus has already done all the work and suffering. There is nothing left for you to pay. There is nothing left for you to earn.

A regular routine of repentance will rejuvenate you as you run. You will be reenergized by the Holy Spirit. He will reveal your sin with conviction. He will help you turn from that sin with mind, heart, and spirit. He will apply once more the love, mercy, forgiveness, and righteousness of Jesus to your tired and aching heart so you can move forward in obedience.

Life is also like a prizefight. You go mano a mano against the ruthless tag-team partners of sin, Satan, and death. The greatest threat to your winning the fight is you. Within you lives the residue from your old nature that wants independence from God. What makes this fight so challenging is that you will constantly have to fight against your old self. You are potentially a contestant divided against himself: the old you and the new you at war. The way you disable the old you so the new you can prevail is by faith. With each punch, you put off the old self and his destructive habits and desires by believing in the truth of who you are in Jesus.

Satan, too, will oppose you as you fight. His strategy will be to discourage and dishearten you through doubt. He will relentlessly oppose you through hard circumstances and through temptation toward hard-heartedness. As he pummels you, he is working toward his greater goal of getting you to doubt God's good intentions toward you in Jesus. All will be lost if Jesus isn't good.

Satan is already a defeated foe.

But Satan is already a defeated foe. Jesus has vanquished him through his perfect life, substitutionary death, and victorious resurrection. As Satan appears in the octagon, your best move is to dismiss him from the fight as one who has already lost to your Champion, Jesus. Don't fall for his deception. Don't move into his ambush.

Last, death will attempt to choke the air from your body through fear. You may find yourself in a brutal headlock at times, paralyzed by the prospect of an inevitable death approaching. But in this vulnerable moment, you must remember that Jesus died to sin so you don't have to. Eternal life has begun for you. It's already happening within you, like water springing up in your soul. This type of life, defined by Jesus as personally knowing God the Father and his Son, never ends from the moment you receive it (see John 17:3). Eternal life is an unbroken experience. No interruption. For as long as you live on earth, you will be indwelt by the Holy Spirit. Then when you pass from this world to the next, Jesus will be there to receive you. There is nothing to fear. You aren't alone, so fight with tenacity and boldness. You win because Jesus already has prevailed.

So What Now?

Live each and every day of your life with your very last day in mind. How will you finish your race? That mostly will be determined by how you live right now. Live in the power of the Holy Spirit. Live as Jesus lived. When your life is finished, you will join all those who receive the crown of righteousness. Run your race. Fight your fight. Keep the faith. Jesus is with you. Through him you most certainly will win.

EPILOGUE

Dear Son,

Not an hour passes that I don't think about you.
I constantly wonder what it might be like if you were
here today. Would you be tall? Would you look like me
or your mom or some combination of the two of us?
How would you get along with your sisters? Most days,
I think about what it might be like to have another man
in our family. But mostly, I try to get my head and heart
around what it might have been like to share my life
with you, my son.

My dad built a close relationship with me around
our common love for the outdoors and sports. We
would fish and hunt together as often as we could.
We never missed a Dallas Cowboys football game on
TV. Ever. We went to University of New Mexico Lobos
basketball games in person. They were a blast. I even

picked Dad's team over Mom's in our baseball civil war, choosing the Yankees over the Dodgers.

Once my dad and I became Christians, we built an even stronger relationship around Jesus, the Bible, and the church. Living down the street from him while I raised my family was a highlight of my life. He was my biggest fan, my closest adviser, and my best friend. Now that we are a thousand miles away from each other, I miss him terribly.

I always thought I would have a son I could share my life with like I did with my dad. Even today when I look at Facebook photos of dads with their boys, I feel empty. On darker days, I just feel broken. Like I will never be whole enough to love your mom or your sisters in the way they deserve because I can't stop hurting over losing you.

Your mom and sisters miss you too. Especially as we celebrate your birthday each year and dream about who you would be if you were still living. We cry a lot. We recommit to loving each other better in the next year. Losing you has made us all appreciate each other more.

Your grandparents miss you too. They send us gifts on your birthday. Jesus has blessed each of them with lots of grandchildren who love and respect them. But they, too, have a hole in their hearts like I do. No matter how many more grandchildren are added, one will always be missing: you.

Son, no one will ever replace you. I am blessed with four amazing daughters. I am a father. But I am also a sonless father in a way I wouldn't have been if you hadn't died. It hurts still and I miss you. I would have considered myself a sonless father for the rest of my life had Jesus not given me a surprise gift. While I was going about my work as a pastor, Jesus graciously brought to me some young men who were without fathers. In a way only he could have arranged, a sonless father became a father to some fatherless sons.

One young man, Greg, captured this surprising gift from Jesus through a letter he wrote when I left him in Albuquerque to serve the church in Seattle:

Pastor Dave,

It felt like my dad wasn't really around much when I was growing up. My memory of childhood is that he would work all day and escape in the evenings into projects or TV. When my parents got divorced, it felt like he virtually disappeared from my life. He was there in name but not in person.

With this void in my life, I've tried to have other father figures. None of them could ever fill the void that the Father does in my life, but I would attribute the role of my spiritual father to you, Dave.

I feel like when Shannon and I first came to City on a Hill, you took me under your wing. I was young and ambitious, but I lacked wisdom and guidance. You have always been there to encourage me and guide me.

Like a father, you have always looked for ways to help me grow. We were only at City on a Hill for a few months when you first let me preach. You pursued me to go through the Missional Church Planting book. You pursued me to go through Shepherd U. You got me the opportunity to go through ReTrain. You have always pushed me to be a better minister.

Like a father, you have pushed me to be a better husband. I remember early on at City on a Hill I was making church my mistress. Shannon was still hurt from our previous church, and she was disassociating herself from City on a Hill. You lovingly corrected me and pointed me to love Shannon before the church.

Like a father, you showed me how to have Jesus as the first love in my life. Your passion for Jesus and his Word has always spurred me on. You consistently asked me about my relationship with Jesus and encouraged me in my walk. You have prayed with me and for me and for my family.

It has been through your influence in my life that Jesus has made me the man, husband, and father I am today. I'll never fully be able to put into words the impact that you have had on my life. It's for that reason we added your name as one of Mason's middle names. Your fatherly legacy will live on through me and my children and hopefully one day their children.

To the glory of God,
Greg Qualls

David, when I read this letter, so many things came together for me that I had been trying to grasp since you died. Although I lost my dearest and only son, God has given me many spiritual sons who have brought so much meaning and joy to my life. In some way, this must have been how Paul felt toward Timothy and Titus. It would explain the affection and concern he had for these men.

Son, my life moves forward without you but also toward you. You are with Jesus, and someday, I will be too. As you worship him perfectly, I strive to do the same. Until we meet again, I will find joy in him. I will find deep satisfaction and fulfillment in being a husband and father and now a father-in-law. My ministry beyond my first flock, my biological and spiritual family, will be to the fatherless sons Jesus has been so good to give to me, a sonless father.

More than anything else, I hope this book has brought glory to Jesus. After that, I hope some fatherless sons have been well served. I owe much to so many of them. They are redeeming a terrible loss for me. They are making me less and less a sonless father with each step of faith they take.

I love you, David, always and forever,

Dad

ACKNOWLEDGMENTS

Thank you, Tyndale House, for taking on this project. I've never written a book before. You have taken a risk with me that I pray is rewarded. You have taught me, encouraged me, and challenged me along the way. I especially appreciate the efforts of Jon Farrar, Senior Acquisitions Editor, and Jane Vogel, Associate Copy Editor. Jon, you have given me clarity about the audience for this book. Jane, the questions you have asked throughout the process have been invaluable and have refined my thinking more than you may know.

Thank you, Mars Hill Church! I love you very much. While I hope this book may help others, I wrote it mostly to you. It is a joy to grow with you as a Christian, a husband, a dad, and a pastor. Your profound love for Jesus, the Bible, our church, and the people among us who don't yet know him is inspiring.

Thank you, Mars Hill staff members, for helping me write this book. John Weston, you were the values keeper for this work. Thanks for tenaciously holding the line. Thank you, Ryan Dorn and Matt Johnson, for looking at my manuscript and working hard to make it readable and true to the gospel.

Thank you, Pastor Sutton Turner. Your passion for good steward-ship has provided me with the time and resources to write this book while first serving Mars Hill. You are to me "a friend that sticks closer than a brother" (Proverbs 18:24).

Thank you, Pastor Mark Driscoll. You have taught me more about what the Bible has to say about being a man than anyone else. This story may be mine, but this book is your idea, and I hope you see your strong influence in its pages. I am grateful and honored to labor with you. You too are a "friend that sticks closer than a brother." I hope I am the same for you.

Thank you, Dad. I am the most fortunate son in the world. You are the strongest man I have ever known, and the kindest man I have ever met. I hope to someday be the man that you are.

Thank you, Lisa, Lauren, Jennifer, and Jillian. You are my joy! When you were younger, people would see us in public and say to me, "Wow, I bet you wish you had a boy in your home!" I would always reply, "I have a son in heaven and my heart and home is full." I hope this book shapes the men you someday marry.

Thank you, Kara. You always said I would write a book. I told you I never would. As is usually the case, you were right! I love you more with each new season of life. You are my best friend. You are an amazing helper. And you are the most devoted follower of Jesus I have ever known.

Thank you, Lord Jesus. You are the only true model for what it means to be a man. And you are the only real means by which men can become who God intended us to be. This book is yours. Do with it whatever you'd like so that your fame grows.

ABOUT THE AUTHOR

Dave Bruskas serves as an executive elder of Mars Hill Church. He is the teaching pastor, overseeing all lead pastors at each Mars Hill location. Born in Albuquerque, Dave planted City on a Hill Church in his hometown in 2001. He pastored that church for ten years before transitioning into Mars Hill Albuquerque, the first Mars Hill outside of the state of Washington. He remained lead pastor until moving to Seattle in 2011 to take on the role of executive elder. He's a graduate of Texas Tech University and Dallas Theological Seminary, where he won the Harry A. Ironside Award for Expository Preaching. He's a proven, seasoned pastor and gifted teacher. He frequently teaches at all Mars Hill locations. He's married to his wife, Kara, and has four lovely daughters.

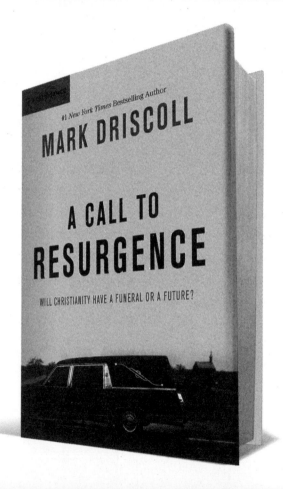